Dedication

To our children Donald, Joseph, Thomas, William, Gracie, and Dixie: We wrote this book with you in our hearts and minds. Choosing the right lifetime partner is only the first step; making it last is the work. We hope that we instilled in all of you the balance of love, intellect, emotion, and empathy that will help you sustain one of life's greatest joys and challenges: a relationship that is loving and brings you happiness that you could have never imagined.

Table of Contents

FAMILY ADVOCATES INFORMATION AND RESOURCES, INC.
www.fairnys.org

Funds these services:

- Help with Parental Alienation
- Help with False Accusations
- Parenting Classes
- Co-Parenting
- Mediating Family Issues
- Mediating Divorces and Separations
- Marital Counseling
- Post Divorce Counseling
- Family Counseling
- Pro Se Help
- Psychological Evaluations
- Forensics
- Mental Health Expert Witness Available
- Referrals
- Attorney Referrals
- Psychological Referrals
- Support Group Referrals
- Court Support (accompanied by an advocate)

A percentage of the proceeds from this book will be donated to help families.

Don Desroches, CDM
Dana Greco, LCSW-R, CDM

Conscious Coupling

POSITIVE INSIGHTS FOR
LONG-LASTING RELATIONSHIPS
SHARED BY TWO DIVORCE
MEDIATORS

ISBN-13: 978-1-940262-75-8

Book editing, interior design, and layout: Janice Taylor
Cover design: Suzanne Lawing

Published by Clovercroft Publishing
Franklin, Tennessee

Clovercroft Publishing

♀ ♂
DANA & DON

Introduction

Most adults would agree that having a fulfilling relationship is extremely important to them. If you are married or are thinking about marriage, you should know that almost half of marriages end in divorce. Out of the half who do stay together, how many couples do you think are really fully satisfied? Do you ever wonder why there are so many unhappy couples? Everyone goes into their marriage confident about the choice they made and believes in their future life together. Traditional marriage vows profess, "Till death do us part," but it seems that, as we see in our mediation practice, couples are now professing, "Till unhappiness do us part."

As certified divorce mediators and through our own personal experiences, we see and deal with a number of couples in pain after deciding to end their marriages. Dana is a licensed family and couples therapist, and together we resolved, as divorce mediators, that we would help people stay out of the court system if they did decide to dissolve their marriages, reducing the conflict and bitterness that ensues in a litigious proceeding. Preferably, however, we resolved to help divorcing couples and their families restructure their relationships because we believe that even though marriages may end, families are forever.

After a number of years of mediating divorces, we needed to get the word out to a broader audience and help even more people with their relationships, so we produced the "New Beginnings" radio show. During this time, with the feedback we received from our audience and followers, we knew that the next step was to write a book to prevent relationships from heading down the path to divorce because our pro-family passion and mission aligns with being advocates to married couples, divorcing couples, children of divorce, and the like.

We treat families on pre- and post-divorce issues and help people restructure their lives and their families. Having treated thousands of families, we thought there must be a way to use our knowledge to help people understand the challenges they would face in their relationships before it was too late. We believe that providing the tools to become aware of those efforts and challenges would help minimize the conflicts in the marriage and ultimately prevent divorce. Obviously, even if you are not married and want to be in a fulfilling and meaningful relationship, these tools would work for you as well.

We were extremely curious about the real underlying issues of why couples divorce, and we came up with a methodology called "Root Cause Analysis" in order get to the real problem instead of the symptoms that people see and the behaviors that are hurtful. The Root Cause Analysis methodology is the process of asking a series of questions until you get to the root of the problem. For example, if someone has left the marriage emotionally, we ask the question "Why?" They may say they left because they did not feel loved by their partner. Then we ask why they did not feel loved, and they may say they were not getting enough quality time with their spouse. Then we ask why they did not get quality time, and it may be because the other spouse was angry at them or felt betrayed because they were not getting a need met. We continue this process of delving deeper and deeper until there are no more questions to ask and we have come to the root of the issue, which may be money values or any one of the other topics in our book.

You may have experienced this if you and your partner ever attended couples counseling, which may have left you still feeling betrayed, angry, or disillusioned about your relationship. That means the treatment and interventions you received skipped over the Root Cause Analysis methodology, which we truly believe is the only real intervention. We have offered RCA to couples, and despite their decisions to end or to work on their relationships, all our couples came away from our sessions with a completely new perspective about their own responsibilities to their relationship, thereby feeling empowered and more in control of their present situation and leading them on the track of self-assurance, confidence, and empathy for themselves and their partners.

We truly believe that the Root Cause Analysis methodology is the only real intervention in couples counseling.

When thinking about a title for this book, we thought the term Conscious Coupling would be an ideal title because of the necessity of being conscious and aware of each other and the relationship to ensure that the couple creates their future together rather than merely allowing it to happen to them. The first step in making any changes is, at a minimum, being aware of the issues or future issues. Only at that time can you make shifts in your perception.

There are thousands of books out there about relationships, and we know that each one offers some value. However, many of these books do not address the conscious level that is needed. Albert Einstein once said, "Problems cannot be solved at the same level of awareness that created them." Therefore you must become conscious or aware of the root problem. Awareness is consciousness and hence the term Conscious Coupling. Conscious Coupling is the awareness that both individuals in the relationship, not just one, have about themselves, each other, and the relationship, as three entities. All three need care and nurturing, and if any one of the three is neglected, then all three will starve and deteriorate.

We wrote this book because both of us felt that a perspective from a mediator's point of view would help couples better understand and grasp the meaning of a committed and truly intimate relationship.

> **We wrote this book because both of us felt that a perspective from a mediator's point of view would help couples better understand and grasp the meaning of a committed and truly intimate relationship.**

We know what it's like to feel that you have met the person you want to spend the rest of your live with. Upon looking at your relationship, you are reminded of all the wonderful attributes your partner embodies and the potential of happiness and fulfillment that lies ahead. We want this happiness and fulfillment for you, but we also want you to know there is work and effort in order to maintain this for years ahead.

We do not believe that most couples are truly conscious when they prepare to commit to one another, which is why we want you to take the time to read and share these concepts with your partner. If only one of you reads this, it will not be enough. One side cannot be conscious while the other is not. That would be the same as driving a car on two tires rather than four or flying an airplane with one wing. In order for your relationship to have the depth and staying power, you both will need to be conscious.

In order to be conscious and involved in Conscious Coupling, it is important that you do a Root Cause Analysis, as we mentioned before. This is a very important component to any relationship. You may have heard this term in business, but it also refers to the organized methodology and thinking to determine the "root" of the work required in a relationship.

By contracting with your partner and professing your love and commitment, you are also contracting that you will maintain your loyalty and effort in keeping the union and bond safe between each of you and developing goals and objectives toward a successful outcome.

This may not sound romantic, passionate, or even sexy, but we want you to have all of that and more. On the contrary, through Conscious Coupling, you can be guaranteed the best sex, romance, and passion you could ever dream possible.

Through Conscious Coupling, you can be guaranteed the best sex, romance, and passion you could ever dream possible.

As we said earlier, Root Cause Analysis is a process of continuing to ask questions until you find the ultimate reason for any dissent or conflict. The concepts offered in this book will challenge you to become a deeper, more enriched couple. Much like the iceberg, although you only see the top that appears above the surface, you know there are miles of the iceberg's bulk hidden beneath that visible tip. Your relationship has the ability to have a depth far beneath the surface of what you see and share and what others see and observe. In those depths is found the greater part of the relationship, and this is where we want you both to travel, below the surface.

As mediators, we often—actually, we always—see the sadness and despair of a deteriorating relationship, if not already deteriorated. We sit across from couples who have lived together for many years, married, with children, lives, friends, extended family that are now all coming to an end and will forever be changed. We want to prevent this despair, and in order to do this, what we are offering is a new way of thinking and an opportunity to build the foundation of your relationship from a very conscious basis.

We want to prevent this despair, and in order to do this, what we are offering is a new way of thinking and an opportunity to build the foundation of your relationship from a very conscious basis.

Approached with honesty with yourself and your partner, it's important to delve into the concept of "root cause" and pull back the layers that lie beneath you, your partner, and your relationship.

The couples that we work with come to us with this belief that they never knew how unhappy their spouses had been in the marriage. They sit across from us and scream out to their spouses things like, "Why didn't you say something!" or "How can you leave me like this? I feel so betrayed!"

If the partner wonders "how this could possibly have happened right before our eyes," we question whether one or either was ever awake. Clearly someone or both had been asleep not to see what was happening and what was deteriorating. We believe, and we want you to also believe, that being married, sharing a life and children, and faking happiness for that long is not humanly possible. We want you to believe and be honest with yourself that if you and your partner had been conscious, it would have been obvious to you that the marriage had severe problems and someone was not happy, while the other was witnessing the problems but failed to say anything.

Conscious Coupling is about starting your relationship with **honesty** and **integrity**. With these two values working and rotating side by side, both of you will build the foundation as solid as the iceberg, but certainly not as cold.

It's unfortunate to reach the point of deterioration when the betrayed partner grieves the loss of their marriage—much of the time silently and by then too late—desperately trying to reconcile or, in bewilderment, figure out what when wrong, when it went wrong, and how they ended up here. It pains us as mediators to witness the brokenness.

As mediators and as a couples therapist, moving a couple along the painful, rocky torment of dissolutionment takes tender words and compassion. However, it also requires honesty and facing of facts that he or she must accept as reality that this breakdown of a marriage was long ago visible, with flags and symptoms clear and big. Yet the fear or anxiety of the partner addressing such flags and symptoms is the very reason the demise occurred.

In order to avoid this very ugly collective experience, the courage to be honest and observant starts at the onset of the partnership. Reading this book at the beginning of your relationship may prevent heartache and confusion in the long run. It is never too early to put any relationship on the right track.

It is very difficult sometimes to determine your wants, needs, and expectations. Utilize this book to help become aware of the necessities within yourself and your partner. Utilize it as a guide for a happy and healthy relationship once you think you have found the best person for you, or while you are casually dating and in the selection process. It's OK to get personal with someone you share time with. Utilize the book as a measuring tool for your choice of partners. It is important to note that anything and everything can be rationalized in the beginning, but after the years have gone by and the challenges of marriage creep up, the things you rationalized once before are not so easy to rationalize anymore. They become barriers. Take the time now to understand your partner before you make one of the most important decisions of your life, and if you are already married, then make the decision to do the work. Do it for you, do it for your partner, and do it for your (future) children.

Instead of collaborating on the chapters, we decided we would outline the topics we should write about and each of us would write a chapter on that topic, using our perspectives, opinions, and knowledge, based on each of our professional and personal experiences. This book offers two perspectives on the same topic instead of one collaborative perspective. Some parts of the book may sound like man versus woman, but it is not intended to be. We wrote from our experiences, which may, in some passages, resemble a feminine/masculine idea, but not always. So we ask you not to get trapped in thinking Dana is the female voice and Don is the male voice. Just know we wrote from each of our own perspectives and experiences.

This book is for anyone who wants to be in a meaningful and fulfilling relationship. We want people to be aware instead of just getting on the treadmill of life and walking on through without actually knowing what is happening to them. We use the grazing analogy: If you left a horse on the side of the road, he would continuously graze, eating grass while walking until the end of day. At that point, he might be three miles down the road, doesn't know how he got there, and doesn't even care. Most of us do just graze through life instead of taking control of our lives and our futures. If we are aware and conscious, we can then take steps to make things better for ourselves, and we can then decide where we want to go, instead of being passively led by life happening to us.

Most of us do just graze through life instead of taking control of our lives and our futures. If we are aware and conscious, we can then take steps to make things better for ourselves.

The last thought we will leave you with is the importance of watching the behavior of our partner. It is important that we watch their behavior and ensure that their behavior reflects what is said. Our partner can help us come to the understanding of how we are perceived and behaving and can help us match that behavior to our words. We can't stress enough how important it is to watch behavior.

So be mindful, be safe, and understand how to proceed wisely. READ THIS BOOK! Marriage can be a great joy and benefit, and when two people follow the premarital GPS guidance contained in the following chapters, there is an excellent chance of success. Do the work, make it fun, and become a good statistic. The pendulum can swing both ways, so choose to create the happy-ever-after ending.

Dana and Don

♀ – DANA

1 – Their Stories

Her Story

The relationships we form have much to do with the childhoods we had. We learn from role models, influences, impressions, and perceptions. What we take from these experiences and what we do with them to shape our own lives is up to us. We all have our childhood stories; the following is mine. I will only illustrate the pertinent points that directly reflect the value of this book.

One of my significant defining moments as a child was when my parents separated. I remember going with my mother to the divorce attorney's office. When I think back on those days as a 10-year-old, the somber words I had overheard, all the anger of injustice, and the confusion of legalese still haunt me with a lingering sadness. My first impression of a divorce attorney was the skinny, middle-aged woman with a beehive, sitting in an over-furnished, mahogany-carved office. She sat across this massive desk as though she were on the other side of a midwestern state. I felt small and insignificant. She appeared to me so distant, yet I knew she

> **The relationships we form have much to do with the childhoods we had. What we do with these experiences is up to us.**

was an integral part of my very personal world, which was changing rapidly. That feeling of insignificance remained with me every time we had to meet with her or anyone else representing the family court system. I didn't fool myself into thinking that my family, my life, and my well-being were not just another case to them. My mother, I remember, was anxious, confused, angry, sad, and scared throughout this ordeal. My siblings and I were never quite sure what her mood was going to be from day to day. I recall feeling shame when the attorney looked down at me from her beige high heels. She wasn't about helping my family as much as it was about sticking it to my dad. "Don't worry, Mrs. Greco, we will take him for everything he's got, even his license."

For a while, money in my household became very tight, and my mother was always stressing out about it. Today, years later, I still take a three-and-a-half-minute shower (in my own home) because my mother would scream through the bathroom door, "HURRY UP–the WATER BILL!"

Even though in this country there have been countless divorces and there will be countless more, I will always feel the sadness and emptiness that permeated my dismantled family. There was financial loss, and what could have been, was no longer. The power and control that the family court had over us was demeaning, especially while being referred to only by a docket number.

As a child of divorce, I had mixed feelings about marriage and stability. I grew up disillusioned, although I do believe in love relationships today. But being a child of divorce, my first defense when things get uncomfortable is to throw in the towel. The notion that love lasts is a fallacy; for me, love must be proven and not assumed.

As a child of divorce and the family court system,

my childhood was interrupted with attorneys, court hearings, and judges, and I often overheard heavy discussions between my mother or father and their families; everyone had an opinion, and our family seemed to be the topic of conversation during the holidays. The Grecos were the scar on the mountain. There was a constant buzz of hostility, despair, and vengeance looming in the air —always!— for years.

During one of the custody battles when I was 13 years old, I was ordered by the judge to return back to my mother. I had moved in with my dad for various reasons. I wanted to stay living with him and not return to my mother's house. Yet the judge had the final decision over me, and this did not feel good at all. I remember standing below His Honor's bench, looking up at him and saying, "NO, I'm not going back; I am not a yo-yo." I was scared, courageous, self-determined, and angry. Who was this judge to make that decision over my life? He didn't even know me? He probably didn't even know my name.

I was aware that my mother petitioned for me to return to her, but I just couldn't be uprooted again. So my dad filed for custody, and although I wasn't sure why they had to have a legal arrangement for their own biological child, I patiently waited for the verdict. All along I worried that during the night I would be kidnapped and brought back to my mother. I know she was hurting because I chose to stay with my dad, and I was hurting too, as I missed her. Bitter litigated divorces bring out the ugly in people; there are no winners. I know my parents loved me, but the divorce overshadowed that, leaving me as a pawn or commodity dragged in between the two of them. If it wasn't my father's wrath that I saw, it was the pitiful despair of my mother that I was subjected to. The battle of custody also impacts the child support, meaning that with me on my father's side, my mother received less. Was wanting me about the cash? These thoughts go through a kid's head, especially when they hear the ranting from their parents.

The guilt of the agonizing decision to choose one parent over the other, and the betrayal that I was accused of, in a once-upon-a-time intact family, laid heavy on me. The disconnection of siblings, parental alienation, and communication cutoffs with extended family, scarred for years, is more than any one family can endure. Yet all of these and more happen every day to most litigated divorced families that end up in court. Holidays with the alternative parent were the worst. Because my mother played victim, I was scolded by her family as though this was my fault. Without any words spoken, I still felt the sneers.

It was my parents who decided to end their marriage, but it was we, the children, who bore the bloody battle. How was it that two educated and sophisticated professional adults—my father, a physician and my mother, an artist—made such a mess of our lives? As the smoke settled over the years, as the lawyers pocketed my college tuition, the war wounds remained and were evident when one day my dad, strolling with his cart through the grocery store, passed my mother and her cart down aisle four—once married with three children, now behaving as total strangers.

♂ – DON

2 – Their Stories

His Story

Dana and I thought it would be a good idea if we each described our own stories and our personal reasons for the book. Neither one of us set boundaries about a starting point, so I will start from the beginning, even though that means starting at the age of five in my case. As I discuss my story, I have changed the names so that people from my past will remain anonymous.

My first kiss was with the girl next door, and as I said before, I was five, yes, five years old. Now kissing Nancy at that age did not produce any fireworks, but it did bring up feelings. I considered this the start of my relationships with members of the opposite sex, even though our relationship consisted of just playing together. I asked to kiss her and she said yes. I gave her a little peck on the cheek, but for me, as a five year old, a boundary was crossed and I would never look back. I never really considered Nancy as my girlfriend, but she was the first girl I remember having feelings for. Of course, they were feelings as mature as a five-year-old's, but I do remember feeling butterflies in my stomach.

My next relationship was with a girl I used to see every Sunday, and we would spend the whole Sunday together. I will call her Denise. Denise and I were attached at the hip.

We did everything together, and I really looked forward to seeing her every Sunday. Our families would get together at Alley Pond Park in Queens, NY, and would spend the entire day from sunup to sundown at that park. It was a great memory of mine. We played sports, we played in the woods, we rode bikes together, and we played in the water. I remember exploring and finding tadpoles, frogs, worms, and insects. We never kissed, but I remember her as someone really special to me. She was my girlfriend, and I remember introducing her as my girlfriend. We spent Sundays together, as well as parties and other family events. I think my feelings about women today go back to my first experience with Denise. I know there are men who like very "girly" girls and traditionally feminine women, but what always made me excited was seeing girls and women who were strong and not afraid of anything. Denise did anything and everything I did. I really believe to this day that my foundation for love was created back then, such that it is important for me to be with a woman who is strong and able to do anything I can do. Not that I like women who are overbearing, but I feel this is the reason why I like a woman who is a true partner, on the same level, and not lower or higher than me in status.

My third relationship started with a game of spin the bottle. That's one way to start a relationship. I remember spinning the bottle, and it pointed at Hailey when it stopped. Boy was I nervous. We did not kiss in the open. We had to kiss in the closet, but I don't remember exactly why no one was able to watch. We went into the closet, and I had absolutely no experience or understanding about how to kiss. I didn't know what to expect, and I didn't know how to get started. We started kissing on the lips, and I have to say it was the worst kiss I have ever had, but it was the first time I really tried to kiss a girl. We did kiss, but it was not even close to being romantic. We did start dating after that, in spite of that horrible kiss, and we called it "going out." It did not last that long because her family moved to England after that.

The next two relationships were brief, and I remember that all we would do was to "hang out" together. We would just do homework together, and while there never was any real dating, we used to spend most of the non-school hours together. I ended the first one because a friend had dared me to do so, and the second one ended because she said she was just trying to make another boy in the class jealous. I don't remember caring too much, so I guess we weren't that close.

The sixth relationship started when I was 16 years old, and I would have to say that this was my first real loving relationship. We were inseparable, and I remember things between us being great. We would do anything and everything together. We lost our virginity together, became really good kissers, were best friends, and dated until the end of high school. This was my high-school sweetheart, and there are a lot of memories from this time. We dated for three years, and I have to say she was my best friend. I think that after three years we got bored with each other and decided to see other people. When I look back, I would say that this was the first time I learned about overcoming obstacles, arguing, and compromising while living day to day in a long-term relationship.

After that, I started dating the woman who was to become my first wife. My first wife was bubbly and had a lot of emotions. She always laughed the hardest and cried the loudest. We were also best friends and partners. I remember at age 20 thinking I could commit to her because she had the greatest personality of anyone that I knew. I thought we would always get along because she was a very happy person and we had all the same core beliefs and values. The one thing I didn't realize at 20 years old was that we each would grow and change, and we would both grow in different directions, so when our kids were teenagers and wanted to be with their friends instead of their parents, we both realized that we had nothing in common. I really believe we had great times together; we built a true family and were part of the community in every sense of the word.

The one thing I didn't realize at 20 years old was that we each would grow and change, and we would both grow in different directions.

She tried desperately for me to like the things she wanted, and I tried to sway her in my direction as well. In this relationship of 20 years, I learned how to be a husband and a father to three great kids. We shared in all the good and the bad times. Unfortunately, after the kids were mostly out of the house, it was then that we realized we did not have anything in common except for the kids. Ending this marriage was the hardest thing I have ever done in my life. When I married her, I thought it would last a lifetime. My commitment to this marriage was real, a value I learned from my parents, and I never would have dreamed that we would become so disconnected.

When I started dating my second wife-to-be, I thought I had all the answers. In this time of my life, I thought I knew exactly what I wanted. I knew myself and what I wanted and needed in a relationship. It would be great. I would take everything that I had learned and finally get the partner I always dreamed about. However, things did not turn out the way I had expected. This relationship was a complete mistake. The only thing good that came out of the marriage was my youngest son. I also have a special connection with him that I never had with my other three children. I feel like only now am I getting that special bond with my older sons. This had a lot to do with the fact that I was the breadwinner of my first family and left all the domestic chores and child rearing to my first wife. I coached all of them, and that relationship was special, but I feel that, despite its challenges, raising a small child as a single dad gives me that really close, special tie that neither one of us could ever forget. A little advice: if you are a dad

A little advice: if you are a dad and do get a divorce, fight as hard as you can to keep your child as a significant part of your life and not just for a couple of hours a week.

and do get a divorce, fight as hard as you can to keep your child as a significant part of your life and not just for a couple of hours a week. Being a father is one of the greatest gifts you can be given. There are men who go through their entire lives without having this connection and feeling.

Getting back to my second wife and how we were so very wrong for each other: As we all do, I said the right things, and she said all the right things. We were smitten with love and were not being real. We were both filled with false hope that neither one of us could see past until it was too late. Every red flag that came up, I rationalized away and didn't listen to my gut feelings and instincts. We were not being honest with ourselves. I did not realize how vulnerable I was until after the damage was done. There were many things I learned in this relationship. Never, never, never make serious decisions when you are in a state of vulnerability. I was vulnerable and she was vulnerable, and we did not even know it. This is why it is so important to ensure you are conscious and aware. I also learned to ensure that behavior follows the words. I think most of us say things that we wish, hope, and need, and our own behaviors may not even match because we may want it so badly. Things were great for a number of years, and then came the crash and burn. I did not realize until I was out of the house how toxic that relationship was to my mental and physical health. It took a good few months before I came out of that dark place. Unhealthy love can be deadly, and it's important to really know the person you are with. I really learned a lot from that relationship and learned that I need feedback from people who know me, because once in a relationship, I become blinded by love.

Now that brings me to my last relationship with Dana. First of all, she is a couples therapist. Come on, how could this go wrong? She knows the questions to ask, the behavior to look for, and the red flags, and she believes in using a third party to help you get through rough patches and help you develop as a couple. That alone gives us a huge advantage. Dana has taught me a lot about myself, and I always say to Dana today, we are not just two people, but when we combine our forces, we are three. We are powerhouses separately, but when together, we are more than we could ever be apart. We can work together, play together, and do just about anything together. We are growing at the speed of light. Yes, we have issues; everyone does. We work through those issues by talking to each other in the right way. We are still learning and growing, but we also are trying to experience everything a couple can experience together in the shortest amount of time. Only through experiences can we really learn about each other. You could be dating someone for ten years and still not really know who they are because you always go to the movies, have no tragedy in your lives, and don't talk about meaningful things. You have company wherever you go, but you don't have a close, intimate partner, sharing everything—every feeling and every thought—together. She brings me to new heights I never would have achieved alone, and I do the same for her. I am always looking out for her, and she does the same for me.

Through my relationship experiences, I hope that you may see some shared feelings and understandings in common to help you in the relationship with your partner in life. Remember, you should learn from every experience you have. You will be better for it, and the growth you have in a relationship can be exponential with the right person—a person who can, in time, *become* your soul mate instead of *beginning* as your soul mate from the start.

The growth you have in a relationship can be exponential with the right person—a person who can become your soul mate in time instead of starting off as your soul mate from the beginning.

♀ – DANA

3 – The Future

Do you have what it takes?

So you have decided to focus on the relationship between you and your partner, have you? Are you ready for the work it entails? I agree with relationship expert Dr. John Gray, PhD, author of *Men Are from Mars, Women Are from Venus,* who believes that "there is more than one ideal mate or 'soul mate' for each of us, and there is no perfect one." Those who find healthy relationships discover the secret that our soul mate isn't actually perfect, but rather that that person is "perfect for us, flaws and all." Your partner and you need to naturally share a core interest, first and foremost filled with mutual love, respect, and appreciation for each other's strengths and weaknesses. The two of you coming together as complete, separate people, while additionally joining together as a couple, adds a component to your life that would not otherwise be there, and I mean a positive, inspirational component. It's the idea that the two of you as complete people are better off together than apart, and by this awareness, that there is a very good chance, given the synergy between the two of you, that the love in your hearts, focused on your relationship, can grow and last a lifetime. If it is your joint decision to move ahead and make this your committed one-and-only relationship, then it is also the time to sit down with your partner and make sure you are both willing to do the work. Do you both agree that this will take work? If you think a relationship should be effortless, then you have been misguided. Anything and everything takes effort, even in the best of circumstances.

In order for the relationship to have staying power, you will both need to promise to keep the lines of communication open, and as you read every chapter of this book, you both need to acknowledge its meaning and work toward making each chapter beneficial for you, according to how the two of you want to manage it.

As for the leading experts on relationships, such as Dr. John Gray and Dr. John Gottman, it's essential that you embrace what they have to offer since they have studied this area for decades. Even in our work as mediators and couples and family therapists, we know that every relationship has its own personality and needs. When studying and intervening in areas that need work in your relationship, it's important that the skills and tools offered are tailored toward what works for both of you. There are no textbooks on relationships; each one is unique in its own beauty, like the snowflake. Did you know that there are more than 17 varieties of snow, and not one snowflake is alike? Like this well-known reference to the infinite snowflake formations, it doesn't hurt for me to remind you that your relationship will never be like anyone else's. Do not burden yourself with comparisons on how other relationships look to you. No marriage is perfect, and just when you might think it's perfect, something will challenge it. This is not an alert that the relationship has crashed, that the most perfect moment in your relationship has passed, and that it's downhill from here. The snag only indicates that there is another opportunity for growth.

Take heed in knowing that as long as the base of your relationship is mutual respect, honesty, love, and inspiration, when a bump in the road trips you, a little help and attention on the conflict will bring you both back to the starting point. Think of it as a growth chart. It zigs and zags, but it is always moving upward. Don't look at your relationship like the stock market. If your relationship maintains power in its integrity, it will never plummet.

Think of your relationship like a savings account that you are always depositing into. There will be hefty deposits, and there will be those minimal ones. Security is knowing that it's there when you need it. Think of your relationship as composed of three parts: you, him, and the relationship. What may not work for you this day, may work for him that day. If it doesn't work for either of you, it may just work for the relationship.

Think of your relationship like a savings account that you are always depositing into.

One simple example: there will be invitations to visit family or friends or an event that neither of you are excited about accepting, but it would be in the best interests of the relationship to go, let's say. Then you go. One thing you will learn from this discipline is that when there are children involved, you both may need to put your differences aside and agree that it benefits the children, even though it isn't something you really want to do.

I tell school kids and my own that, when you don't want to do your homework or go to school that day, you must anyway. By maintaining your responsibility when it's not your desire, you build mental muscle. Will kids really use half of the stuff they are taught academically? Not likely. But what they will use is the tenacity they develop in persevering through adversity; in other words, resiliency.

When you or your partner are struggling with adversity, and maybe feel so hopeless that you want to throw in the towel, remember that the real reward is managing to hang in there. Work through the conflict and then assess where you are. Quitting is not an option, unless drugs, alcohol or domestic violence exists.

Couples have come to me to help save their marriages after a discovery of infidelity. This type of betrayal in an intimate, committed relationship is devastating. When a couple recognizes what happened that led one partner to stray, there is pain, but a sense of relief. Not to say that infidelity has any place in a committed relationship, because it absolutely does not. What the infidelity screams is that needs are not being met! If one of you feels that their needs, both personally and relationally, are unfulfilled, the communication must, must be immediately addressed.

Cloe Madanes, a teacher of family therapy, shares with her audience six human needs. They are consistency; inconsistency; love and connection; growth and development; validation; and contribution. Cloe Madanes describes these needs for the purpose of relationship to one another. When two people share these needs relative to the other, their relationship consists of similar values in the same order and priority. Ms. Madanes believes that the more the values match, the stronger the relationship will be. These needs are basic human needs yet the order of priority varies. You may remember, if you have taken a psychology class, the scale of Maslow's Hierarchy of Needs, as determined by the humanistic psychologist Abraham Maslow and written in his 1943 paper "A Theory of Human Motivation." According to Dr. Maslow, the Hierarchy of Needs is diagrammed as a pyramid, starting on the bottom level with **Psychological**: breathing, food, water, sex, sleep, homeostasis, and excretion. The next level above that is **Safety**: security of body, employment, resources, morality, the family, health, and property. Above this level is **Love/ Belonging**: friendship, family, and sexual intimacy. Then above this is **Esteem**: self-esteem, confidence, achievement, respect of others, and respect by others. And it is topped off with: **Self-Actualization**: morality, creativity, spontaneity, problem solving, lack of prejudice, and acceptance of facts. These concepts are always available to explore and research on your own. When inner conflict ensues in you, your partner, or both of you collectively, you may find these ideas helpful in order to dissect what might possibly be wrong in your present situation.

Cohabitation with another human being is the most difficult of all human tasks. Be self-caring and nurturing to yourself and your partner. Address delicate subjects with compassion and balance. Ask for what you need from your partner, and welcome him to ask for what he needs. As long as you both feel safe in this relationship, there can be enough staying power to last a lifetime. So here's your chance to fulfill the goal.

Be self-caring and nurturing to yourself and your partner. Address delicate subjects with compassion and balance. Ask for what you need from your partner, and welcome him to ask for what he needs.

♂ – DON

4 – The Future

Will your marriage be forever?

So you may be thinking about marriage or maybe you're already married. That's great—or is it? Maybe you are, or were, being forced into marriage through an unplanned pregnancy, you have been given an ultimatum, or maybe you are the one who really wants, or wanted, to get married. It's time for a reality check. Now picture this: you have been married for 10 years, you have two children, you have your house in the suburbs with the big screen TV, barbecue in the back, and a deck around the pool. You're living the life. Work is great, and you're feeling good about things. One day you come home from work and are served with divorce papers from your wife. What happened! You thought everything was good. You were bringing home the money, coaching the kids, and doing all the things around the house. You knew there were some bumps and hiccups in the marriage, but everybody has problems. You thought they would be sorted out at some time. Why didn't she just ask for counseling? Or maybe you're wondering, why does she think it's so bad?

Getting served papers in this way never feels good. It immediately puts you on the defensive. You get angry and can't believe this has happened. All sorts of things go through your head. You are thinking: she found somebody else, maybe she is hiding money, and she has been plotting this divorce for a long time. You are just finding out and are immediately put in a bad place. Not only that, you have to be in court within the next 30 days. You scramble to find a lawyer, and when you find one, you discover that you have to deposit $7,500 as a retainer. You really have no idea what this money is going to be spent on, but you sign up because you are desperate and your close friends say this lawyer is great. Now after months of going to court and spending the initial $7,500 after just 20 hours of paperwork, court time, etc., you now have to give the attorney another $7,500. You don't even have it, so you have to reach out to family and borrow the money. Eventually, you either settle and have the lawyers draw up the papers, or you go through an expensive trial after which the judge decides your case. It is ugly: you have to pay $2,000 monthly in maintenance to your now ex-wife because she has been raising the children and not working outside the home, and you have to pay $1,500 in child support. OUCH! Now this really doesn't feel good. The kicker is that you also have to move out of the house and you don't get to see your children, except for every other weekend and maybe one dinner during the week. Now you're saying to yourself, why in hell did I work so hard only to give all the money to this shrew? I have to pay all this money and don't even get to see the kids? You are not in a good place.

Now think back to when this started. You may have been all lovey-dovey, and your wife looked beautiful. She treated you like a king, obviously before the kids came along, and life was looking better than you could have ever imagined. You wanted to work hard to give this person all the good things in life, only to have it come crumbling down. You worked hard, not her; why does she get all that and I get nada, zilch, nothing. What is wrong with this picture! You could imagine the look and frustration of anybody put in this position. If you don't believe there are thousands of people in every state who go through this, just Google "Fathers' Rights," and you will find a boatload of organizations that consistently see these injustices on a regular basis. Do you want to be another statistic and another unhappy dad?

Just Google "Fathers' Rights," and you will find a boatload of organizations that consistently see these injustices on a regular basis.

Some women learn very quickly that the court system and the laws are in their favor, and they work very hard to get you out of the picture when they make up their mind. They want your wallet to stay, but you out the door. They can even go to such extremes as to file an order of protection against you so you cannot see the kids. You think it doesn't happen, but I can show you thousands of cases in which it has. Our justice system rewards the weak and punishes the strong.

NOW THAT YOU HAVE THE TRUE PICTURE, LISTEN UP MY GULLIBLE AND UNSUSPECTING FRIEND! This CAN happen to you. Don't think your relationship is any different than all the other dads who lost custody of their children and have now become the ATM machine for their exes. You think you are smarter than everyone else and your love is stronger than anyone else's, or maybe you are not a pansy and would never let a woman walk all over you. Well think again. Divorce happens to 50% of married couples annually. Also, out of the 50% of non-divorced people, how many do you think stay married and are not happy? Let's just say maybe 10%

to 20% of marriages are happy marriages. Now, out of the 50% who get divorced, 90% of the women get custody and support of the children. How about that for being bleepin' fair? So now do you really believe you have the relationship that will last? Are you one of the 50% who will make their marriage work? Starting to have some doubt? You'd better!

Listen up now, take note, and do all the homework in this book before you put yourself in a position to be the ATM for the family, wherein the family comes to a machine, gets the money they need, and they never need to see you. Also, just so you know, you will probably end up living on the couch at your parent's house. The payments are way too high for men, and they end up defaulting on their payments. So they get their pay garnished at work, and if they owe money, they get their drivers licenses suspended, lose their passport privileges, and can even go to JAIL! Yes, you can go to jail. Imagine having to go to jail because you are a dad. It's hard to believe this happens, but it happens to unsuspecting people daily—people you would never believe, such as doctors and lawyers and other professionals. So you'd better be extremely clear that you are marrying the right woman, NOW, before it's too late. There are some real war stories that I would love to share if I knew it would help you. Feel free to contact me to ask. If you still think you definitely have the right person, read the stories. However, even if you think you have the right person, don't you think it would be wise to take note of the things we have written? OK, let's get started.

> **Listen up now, take note, and do all the homework in this book before you put yourself in a position to be the ATM for the family.**

5 – Marriage

Marriage—Is this really what you want?

My mother freely shares her wisdom when it comes to relationships. She has had two marriages, and from what I have witnessed, she has certainly learned much from them. Daughters could learn a lot from mothers and all women who have embarked on this terrain once or twice, if not as many as the sunsets. One of my mother's strongest opinions is the one she throws out when the topic of marriage comes up—usually at a family gathering, most of the time while celebrating a recent engagement of a cousin or other relative: "We, as women, don't necessarily think the marriage is as important as being proposed to." For the newly engaged couple as well as the rest of us, there's usually an awkward silence. However in all her wisdom, she may have hit on one aspect of this phase in the relationship: the romance of the proposal. "THE proposal." Men plan unique, creative ways to ask their special girl to marry him. We see it everywhere, and hear about it: "Popping the Question." He secretly plants the ring in a champagne glass, or whisks her away on a romantic mountain top, or dines her at her fanciest restaurant, then gets down on one knee before the waiter trips over him. Magical moments to be shared for years to come, if you're fortunate to be with a guy who takes the time to think about this and has the sensitivity and the guts to make it a memorable event because it's suppose to mean something. Personally, I wouldn't know. For my magical moment, my guy at the time turned to me before he stepped into the bathroom one Tuesday morning and said, "Hey you, ya wanna get married– 'cause it's starting to get embarrassing." Did I accept this as my one memorable romantic moment? Yeah, I did, but don't lose respect for me. I got my revenge for his uninspired quest for my hand in marriage–I married him.

My mother and I often talk about men and relationships. Now granted, my mother is the Grand Poobah of the Man Haters Club. It's never easy talking to her about love, but I do listen. She never sent my sister or I into the arms of a man who merely sought to provide and take care of us. She always encouraged my siblings and I to be self-sufficient and independent, and I tell my daughters the same thing, except I don't say it from my appointed seat in the Man Haters Club. For the record, I'm not a member.

I remember that I called my mother and told her the good news about planning a wedding. She was half excited, not because I was moving away from home; that wasn't it. I had been on my own for 14 years already. She liked the idea of a wedding, so that was comforting. Then I mentioned that I liked the idea of a bridal shower–I saw her roll her eyes. I might as well have said I wanted a colonoscopy without the anesthesia. She asked with disgust, *WHY?* Wanting a shower and fanfare led her to worry that I was caught up in the event more than I was in the brutal reality of a marriage. I was in agreement to some extent. The idea is somewhat silly. I had been on my own since age 17 and was now 32 years old, and if I couldn't buy my own toaster by now, I had no business getting married. I now tell my daughters the same thing.

My mother is a fun, artistic, spirited woman, and she was afraid that I was getting swept away by the plans for the wedding day and not my wedded life, projecting into the future soon afterwards that I'd fall into some kind of marital comatose state.

For me, getting married meant that I no longer needed to think about dating or any of that nonsense. I had plenty of time and stories pertaining to that phase. Now, I could focus on my career and other things. Was it about "being settled," or was it "settling"? All I know is that for six straight months after the wedding, from the first day of the honeymoon, I suffered with severe anxiety and panic attacks, clinically known as an adjustment disorder. It was not a brief courtship or shot gun wedding; we had been living together for four years! I was 32 years old! Aaagh, but the whole idea sent me into a heart-palpitating, forehead-sweating, up-half-the-night, six-month nightmare. Never had I ever experienced such a condition. And then one day the anxiety ended, and I settled into married life in the heart of Greenwich Village, where now I felt I was too old to live. Married life changes the way you feel about yourself; it's very adult. Or at least it's meant to be.

Was getting married about "being settled," or was it "settling"? Do women marry because it validates us as women?

Why do women want to marry? Is it because we need someone out there to ask for our hand in marriage? Does it validate us as women? Or are we delusional in thinking that marriage is for the princess within us.

I recently found my wedding dress in an old trunk. I thought I had thrown that away years ago. When I found it, I immediately tried it on. As I zipped it up with ease—and with a big relief, mind you—it was a little lose. Yay! My 19-year-old walked into the apartment and caught me. "Oh God," she exclaimed, "you're not getting married again are you?"

"NO, why would I? You're here already, and that's all I need. I'm plenty happy as it is, but thanks for your interest and concern,"

What is it with the females in my life? Doesn't anyone endorse me as a wife? But for all of you thinking seriously about this step—maybe the first time, maybe the second or third—do you feel pressured into getting married? Is it starting to get embarrassing not to be married? Are you thinking about marriage because you want to settle down or are you settling?

Have you dated enough in your life? I believe dating a fair variety of men is important. In fact, your twenties are for dating—perhaps all the wrong people, as I believe—because by the end of the dating phase you have a very good sense of what you are looking for and what you are not. Know this one thing and hold it true to your belief: men are designed to sow their seeds; we, as women, are designed to select that seed. Select carefully.

> **"Men marry women and hope they will never change, and women marry men and hope they will change. Inevitably, both are disappointed."**
> *– Einstein*

You are not going to change that man either. Sure, he may evolve a centimeter, but that's about it. Don't expect much more. What you see is what you get. Einstein said a lot of interesting things, but you should listen to what he once stated: "Men marry women and hope they will never change, and women marry men and hope they will change. Inevitably, both are disappointed." He wasn't known as a genius for nothing.

If you hold on to the notion that once you're married your man will grow up, or be more responsible, or act more like the adult—but right now he is none of these—then brace yourself. Just because he has a gold band around his finger and said "I do" only means he has a gold band around his finger and muttered (I know, I know with a tear in his eye, spare me) "I do." It does not give him super powers to launch him into the husband-sphere.

I realize I sound like my mother now, as an enrolled member of the Man Haters Club, but trust me, it's going to save you the heartache later on if you just enter into marriage realistically. It sounds like what I'm saying is that when you get married, the growth and development clock stops. Instead I am saying that there is room for growth, but the basis of his personality, values, and whatever happened in his childhood won't change. They will only become more pronounced as you get to know him and lie with him.

We want to believe that marrying our mate is going to bring us the truest gift of all, happiness ever after. Or at least make life more meaningful.

If you want to get married because you feel you are getting too old or the biological clock within your uterus is getting restless, but you're not exactly sure about marrying this particular guy, then take the money you were going to spend on your dress, and go down to the nearest sperm bank. If you are looking to be a mother more than a wife, be honest enough with yourself. When you become a mother and you are not in love with your husband, the love affair quickly becomes one between you and your child, leaving the guy out in the cold, angry, and feeling betrayed.

Know what it is that motivates you to wanting to be married:

- Is it about children?

- Is it to keep up with your friends who are married? Is it because your younger sister is getting married before you, and now you are the "spinster"?

- Are you marrying for financial security? If so, eventually the motive will reveal itself when money seems to be a hot button.

- Are you marrying this man because, no matter what, he will always be your best friend, your most intimate confidant, your lover in all the definitions of intimacy: romantic love, familial love, erotic love, right down to sex-for-the-sake-of-sex partner?

- Do you love this man enough to know that when you fall out of love on occasion you will commit to returning back to love?

- Will you love this man when he loses his job and his confidence and it takes him months or maybe years to find a new one?

- Will you love this man when he disappoints you for the fiftieth time, even though you have explained to him, with tears, what he does that hurts your feelings and still he behaves badly?

- Will you love this man and honor him even when the temptation of the Man Haters Club members finds you whirling with agony and frustration and they lure you to join their club, but that would mean divorcing your husband?

- Will you love, honor, and appreciate his strengths and

find his flaws surmountable rather than holding them against him and tracking his mistakes like a road map? Searching out every mistake like it is a point of interest on a travel log? Making one mistake an event that he can never live down? Will you?

- Or will you get pleasure out of bossing him around, making him go where you want to go, not where he wants to go because you don't? Bossing him and controlling him until you have no respect for him and then yelling at him for not having a backbone? Will you marry this guy and teach him to fear you until he broaches any delicate topic as though he's stepping onto a minefield? And you like it that way, but then you lament about the relationship because he never talks to you? All as you complain to your therapist with confusion.

- Do you see him as a little boy who needs nurturing? And if you didn't marry him, he'd be devastated? Trust me, he will be fine; so don't think you are saving this guy from a life of loneliness. They quickly recover, faster than women.

- Or are you marrying this guy because you have done such good work on him you will be damned to lose him to someone else and have them benefit from all of your work? If you think you've sculpted your own version of Michelangelo's David but you don't really see yourself spending the rest of your life with him, then let him go. I'm sure your creation will be worked over anyway. And as for finding new love that is truly a long-lasting and better relationship that works for you, more than the one you let go, you will still have the opportunity for artistic expression.

Why are you motivated to get married? Take the time to explore your feelings. If anxiety rushes in along with the fear of accepting that this might not be the one, then picture yourself moving on without him. But if this is not the result of exploring your feelings and he IS the one, then congratulations, you are ready to use this book: take notes, use a highlighter, refer back to it, and keep it to browse through on your tenth, your twentieth, and many more anniversaries of the day you picked this book off the shelf. Mark the day, because this is the day when you took your relationship, in whatever its present state, to the beginning of a mountain climb, heading toward the summit of sweetness known as YOUR GREATEST RELATIONSHIP EVER.

♂ – DON

6 – Marriage

Do you know why you want to marry?

People get into a relationship for many different reasons. Do you know your motives for being in a relationship or for getting married? This is extremely important because if they are not the right reasons, you surely will have issues in the future. The following is a list of bad and good reasons for getting into or staying in a relationship and why.

WRONG REASONS FOR A RELATIONSHIP

1. **You can't be alone:** There are people who cannot be by themselves, and this tends to be the biggest reason why people get into relationships for the wrong reasons. Be honest with yourself and make sure this is not the reason why you need to be with someone. That does not mean it's bad to want to be with other people; it means you get anxious when you are alone. You need to be comfortable with yourself, by yourself, and enjoy time alone.

2. **Pressure from family and friends:** Some people feel the need to have a relationship because there is pressure from family members that they need a significant other to be complete. Also, you may want to be in a

relationship because all of your friends have a partner or they are all married or married with kids and you want to stay connected. While being in a relationship can be a great thing, you need to be in it for your own good reasons and not because family and friends are pressuring you to do so.

3. **To solve your problems:** If you have issues in your life and are trying to solve them by having someone else in your life, think again. You need to be a whole person in order to make a relationship a solid one. This means you need to be healthy mentally, spiritually, physically, and emotionally. You cannot be an alcoholic and expect someone to help you out of it; nor be rebounding from a relationship, have a mental illness, be in need of financial support, in need of giving financial support, or stuck as a single parent. Having someone else in your life may help in the short term, but it will not provide you with a healthy relationship.

4. **For sex or intimacy:** Some people get into a relationship to have more sex or more intimacy. They just want the warm body of another person. Although this can feel good, it does not provide you with a healthy and sustaining relationship.

5. **Your need to win the challenge or have the "Trophy":** You are looking for the trophy girlfriend. Someone whom everyone looks at and says, "Wow, you really got lucky." This may be great for Barbie and Ken, but not for a serious, mature relationship.

6. **As a temporary solution:** Some people get together because of·the fringe benefits and perks or just because they want to be spontaneous or are very impulsive

people. For obvious reasons, this is not good for a long-lasting union and bond. However, if both of you understand this, then it could be OK since you know that's all it is.

7. **Thinking nobody else wants you:** You would only feel this way if you have low self-esteem. You need to get this out of your head as soon as possible. There are always other people, and you just need to get out and date or, even better, get out and engage in an activity that makes you feel alive. This is where you will meet people who have the same interests as you. Having the same interests is a huge part of keeping the relationship strong and healthy.

8. **For the children:** This is a difficult thing to decide, but it is important for you to be happy, and if you are happy, you will be a better person for the children. It is also better for the children to see you in a healthy relationship instead of a miserable one. You are setting an example for them, whether good or bad, and you don't want them to get into bad relationships themselves.

GOOD REASONS FOR A RELATIONSHIP

1. **Health:** It has been proven that married people live longer and are happier. We feel good when doing nice things for our partner and having that person do nice things for us.

2. **Goals:** It is easier to achieve goals when you have a partner with the same goals or, at a minimum, who is working with you to help you achieve yours. That partner provides another set of eyes, another head, another set of hands and sometimes can help motivate us when we have hit a brick wall or have stalled. When

you do things and have them appreciated, it motivates you to do more. Also, when things go wrong, there is someone who can pick you up and vice versa.

3. **Fun and laughter:** It can be a lot of fun to enjoy moments in life with someone else, creating memories together that can last a lifetime. What better than to laugh and have jokes that only relate to you two? The fun memories you create will not only last a lifetime, they will cement your relationship.

4. **Romance, cuddling, sex, and intimacy:** Having a partner who enjoys the same level of romance, cuddling, sex, and intimacy can help you go far. This will make you happier, give you more energy, and create a warmth within. If you take the time to grow with your partner and learn what she likes sexually and romantically, it can be enlightening and thrilling.

5. **Taking walks and holding hands:** This is just an extension of the romance. It gives you that fulfilling feeling of having someone by your side through thick and thin.

6. **Cooking partner:** Having someone to cook with, finding new recipes and enjoying the different flavors, can be exciting and a great adventure.

7. **Acceptance:** Having someone who accepts you for who you are, with all your quirks, can be very uplifting, helps you enjoy life, and improves your ability to laugh at yourself.

8. **Grow with someone:** What is better than being able to heal yourself, grow as a person, and learn new things about yourself, all with the help of a partner. You also get to help that partner grow as well. It is easier to learn things about yourself when you have someone who

loves you and helps you grow by telling you things that no one else would tell you. It could be good or bad, but it is the feedback each of us needs sometimes to personally develop and grow.

I hope you took the time to read through the right and the wrong reasons to be in a relationship. You need to identify the ones that hold true for you and your partner. Why are both of you in this? Knowing why you do what you do and being OK with it is the first step. If you don't like the reasons you are in a relationship, then make some improvements and turn those things around.

♀ – DANA

7 – Trust

Is he trustworthy?

When we were researching this book, we surveyed many couples who were in relationships for varying lengths of time: some over thirty years and some who were together for less than a year. To the question, "What is the key to a successful relationship?" the number one answer shared by all was TRUST—except for the few who said fear, but we think they were just kidding.

Without trust as the infrastructure in a relationship, that relationship's stability is questionable. However, trust cannot be discovered in the relationship between two people; it must be earned. If trust is broken, its repair and rebuilding takes much more work and commitment. Unfortunately, many relationships have ended due to the inability to rebuild that trust. Therefore, when the relationship is forming, pay close attention to the component that is its glue: trust. This is the core of a happy, healthy union.

> **Without trust as the infrastructure in a relationship, that relationship's stability is questionable.**

Trust is not only about faithfulness within the intimate layers of your relationship, but also in t h e outward expression of its unity. But when the relationship has experienced an infidelity and betrayal, the devastation can destroy every part of the relationship. More about infidelity is addressed later in this chapter as well as in the "Sex" chapter, "How Do You Keep the Flame Burning?"

There are many variables in the relationship that indicate and measure the trust within the couple's commitment. Even before the relationship becomes exclusive, one or both of you are paying attention to how your partner responds to you and their reliability. Have you been in other relationships that have compromised trust? If you were in a relationship with someone who betrayed your trust, you are going to be on guard with the next one. When trust is broken in one relationship, it's very easy to be suspicious of everyone else who comes along. I'm sorry if the betrayals of the past have scarred you. But considering that you have learned from the past, you can grieve and move on and start to believe that all relationships don't have to be hurtful or deceitful. Knowing more will only benefit you the next time.

By paying attention to the behaviors of your partner, you will be more self-assured in knowing and predicting whether you and your partner will be trustworthy:

1. Let's start with consistency in keeping to our word. For example, in the early stages of the relationship when plans are being made, do you or your partner change the plans on a whim, maybe thinking that the other wouldn't mind? When this occurs, the unpredictability can set a tone that causes undue stress in the relationship, even if it is as minor as suddenly switching a plan of going out for dinner. Perhaps when he picks you up, you tell him that you aren't very hungry and are no longer interested in going out.

2. Another example is his mood. If he has mood swings—one minute you are talking to him about his day; then you mention something completely unrelated; and he takes an attitude—this is not good. His unpredictable mood will inhibit your ability to trust him. This goes for both of you. Mood swings on your end will cause him to hesitate in communicating with you, in fear that your unpredictable reactions mean he must be on guard. No one likes to feel they have to tip-toe around a topic or worry that bringing up a subject will turn into a major argument. Mood stability is a necessary trait for a couple to feel safe enough to talk about issues that may cause defensiveness, hurt feelings, or confusion.

3. One of the best ways to know that you are in a trusting relationship is by being able to say no when you feel strongly about something and need to disagree. You sometimes feel that it is best for the relationship if you try to compromise or be flexible. And as relationship experts suggest, this is true. Flexibility in a relationship is needed in order for both of you to share and meet needs. However, when you are not being honest with yourself or your partner, then trust is being compromised. Being honest and expressing genuine feelings at all times allows for your partner to feel safe that feelings are openly expressed and clear communication is the priority. So if you mean NO, say NO; if you mean YES, say YES.

4. Having belief in your partner's capabilities will help build layers of trust. Couples who find fault with each other's skills or strengths will chip away at trust with their criticism.

5. Being open and trusting in a relationship fosters inti-

macy. Intimacy is about vulnerability and trust. The way in which you both will deepen your intimacy is by being open in your expression. Expressing honesty in what you feel and in the individual and collective needs of each of you will securely position the relationship on solid ground. Neither one of you will wonder what the other is thinking or feeling when it comes to being unfulfilled, disappointed, elated, or curious. This can sound like it takes away the mystery that energizes some people, but believe me, there is plenty of room for mystery and eroticism in your relationship. In fact the solid foundation of trust can bring the eroticism and mystery to a new, heightened pleasure. In other words, because of trust, this excitement can be more safely explored.

If you are in a loving relationship, neither one of you will want to hurt the other; quite the contrary, you are together to protect each other.

If you or your partner have to guess what you mean or say or need, then it is very difficult for both of you to really trust each other within an intimate commitment. No one likes to feel they need to second-guess what the other one is thinking. This can feel like game playing. Playing games in a committed relationship will cause insecurity and humiliation. If you are in a loving relationship, neither one of you will want to hurt the other; quite the contrary, you are together to protect each other. Once you are consistently being protected and are consistently protecting your partner, you are in a relationship that is trustworthy.

When there has been a betrayal, it is very difficult to repair the trust that both of you have built up. Many couples who have experienced betrayal—such as infidelity, uncovered lies, hidden pasts, abuse, spying, lack of support, broken promises, addictions, and other damages that have impacted the infrastructure of the relationship—have a long road back to trustworthiness. One partner may go outside of the relationship and have an affair; when the spouse discovers this infidelity, it is truly devastating.

Couples who decide to work through this problem can only do so once they are able to talk about how their relationship led to this infidelity in the first place. Even if the revelation was dissected and repaired, it is not foolproof. Many couples will find themselves again at this same place of betrayal. It is an enormous failure between them. If the couple still tries to overcome the collapse and get to the root of the failure, the depth of destruction seems unbearably impossible to comprehend, and the return to a trusting union seems unimaginable. Even if the relationship has the love but not the trust, love alone will not suffice.

Why then do you even wonder how a relationship can even be called a relationship if there lacks trust? This is a good question. Your footing in this relationship and others that may be with friends or family begins to feel unsteady. Being betrayed can affect your own self-esteem. Being untrustworthy and being the betrayer also reflects a low self-esteem. Take stock of who you are and who your partner is.

Do not let the bitterness of this relationship contaminate your other relationships by being suspicious, angry, jaded, or paranoid. Relationships that end because they lack trust or because trust has been broken are relationships that were not fully committed, even though they appeared to be. A relationship that was not fully committed was not based in true love. The "love" that ends up painfully broken by betrayal was never love, but merely LUST.

Lust does not commit; it is selfish; it is short-lived. Love is selfless, fearless, honest, mature, devoted, protecting, respectful, and much more challenging. To give up on finding true love would be a tragedy. Staying safe by limiting your opportunities of finding true love is unwise. If what you thought was love was only lust, then it behooves you to try again. To repair the relationship that has been betrayed will take work to begin again with real LOVE. Just when you think you are in love, think again, and ask yourself how much TRUST you are willing to give him.

If you are in a loving relationship, neither one of you will want to hurt the other; quite the contrary, you are together to protect each other. To give up on finding true love would be a tragedy.

♂ – DON

8 – Trust

Do you believe?

Trust is not an easy thing to pinpoint in a relationship with your partner. Trust in your partner is more than just staying faithful and not disrespecting each other. That subject is covered in the "Infidelity" chapter. No, trust is about feeling that you can be safe with your partner. As guys, we want to be the strong ones; we never want to appear weak; and we never want to be vulnerable to anybody. We are the strong sex and always need to appear strong. Well, I am here to say that you must check your ego at the door. Your ego will only cause trouble in every aspect of your relationship. You can be strong in a lot of ways, but trust and vulnerability are not any of those areas.

Now that does not mean we are supposed to be purposefully weak to show that we are sensitive. No, this is about letting our guard down and being open to our partner about everything. If we do not trust and are not allowed to be vulnerable, then we will never be honest with our partner, and we will never be honest with ourselves. This is a very difficult thing for guys. Society tells us that we are always supposed to be the protectors and we are always supposed to stay strong, even if all the walls are crashing down on us. How would you like to see a gangster movie in which all the gangsters put their vulnerability on display to everyone around them? Yeah, that would be a sight. I think they all would be shot by the end of the movie because they appeared weak. OK, so we may still have to keep our walls up when it comes to other relationships in our lives, including work and public associations. Where we can afford to be vulnerable is with our partner.

At this point, I'm sure you are saying, "There is no way I could be vulnerable with my partner," and there may be many reasons why you say that. They also may be very valid reasons. Let's say your partner is always on the phone with her girlfriends and she tells her close girlfriends every bit of detail about you and your relationship. Also, she may confide in her parents, or at least her mom, about everything.

In order for you to drop your guard, you MUST be with a partner who is trustworthy. You need to be able to tell her anything and everything without it being spilled all over.

Now hear this: in order for you to drop your guard, you MUST be with a partner who is trustworthy. You need to be able to tell her anything and everything without it being spilled all over. If you cannot trust your partner, there is a real problem. Either you have the wrong partner, or your partner will not change, or you have an issue with trust. None of them is any good or will ever help you in your relationship. There will need to be some changes in your life. You absolutely need to have a discussion with your partner about trust. Dana and I have talked to many couples and most of them stated trust as the number one reason for being in their current relationship.

Now some of you may have only been dating for a minimal amount of time and may not have developed that trust yet. That is OK because, with some people, it takes years to fully develop trust. In my opinion, it is a good thing to have your guard up initially until you can naturally and gradually let out that rope of trust. In this way, trust is mutually earned. I think the best way I can describe trust is as a brick wall that has been built high enough that you can peek over it at your partner. She can only see a minor part of you, and you can only see a part of her. Over time, if the relationship is growing, those bricks start to breakdown; you are allowing your partner to see more of you, and you can see more of her. Now you may say, "That doesn't make sense, Don. How can I see more of her when I am the one trusting more?" Well, I'll tell you that as

> **Trust is as a brick wall that has been built high enough that you can peek over it at your partner. Over time, if the relationship is growing, those bricks start to breakdown.**

your trust grows and you trust her more, she will trust you more, and as you become more vulnerable to her, she will become more vulnerable to you. I also want to say that the size of the wall is an individual thing, and as people age, that wall gets taller and taller with the more relationships they have. That's because with every failed relationship, the walls become harder to break down in the next one. Young adults are more trusting, and the walls are not too hard to break down, but when you become mature adults, you become more jaded, more critical, and more skeptical. It is just human nature. Every time you are hurt, more bricks are added to that wall. It is also possible that, while you are in an initially trusting relationship, a wall can emerge and become bigger because of an infidelity or other hurtful experience. So instead of a relationship growing, it is actually shrinking, and trust is diminishing with it.

Now that being said, take a good hard look at your

relationship, and try to see if you have erected walls. This is very difficult because those walls may not be easy to see; you have to have good self-awareness to see them. It is not possible to have the fullness of love with your partner unless you have complete trust in that person. This means you can say anything to her and do anything with her, and it would never be brought back up in a fight, it would never be shared with anyone else, and it would never be used against you if you were ever on bad terms.

Can you be completely honest with your partner about everything? Can you tell her anything and everything that you do? Can you tell her everything that you are thinking? Oh, did I hit a nerve? This may be a place where you really don't feel comfortable, but this is where the good relationships turn into great relationships. When you get to a point at which you can tell your partner all of your thoughts, you have broken down the wall. Maybe you are not comfortable with some of your thoughts, but keeping them inside and not sharing them can make the situation worse. It is really about getting to that core place—the place where that stranger lives. If you let the stranger out, then he is not a stranger any longer. It becomes much easier, and you are freer to enjoy your partner and yourself. When you have the right person and you have developed that mutual trust, then release the inhibition in you. It will feel really great.

I will also tell you that when you fully trust someone to that level and when that trust is held mutually inviolable, the sex is phenomenal! That's right, the trust is brought into the bedroom—either to good advantage in the case of true, mutual trust; or to your disadvantage if you have trusted your partner with certain thoughts and events that she shares with others. Never underestimate the power of trust.

♀ – DANA

9 – Sex

How do you keep the flame burning?

This is a complicated area. And you may need to really reflect on who you are as a woman when it comes to sex. Much of your desire for sex began in early childhood. When you first encountered feelings for another person, say a crush, how did you react? Some girls had crushes all of the time and idolized movie stars and classmates from kindergarten on up. Were you a girl who dreamed about being in love? Was being in love and being in a romantic relationship on your to-do list? Did being desired by others mean anything to you? Or were you one of the girls who secretly had a crush on a boy in school, but you were fearful if he knew, in case you would be laughed at or rejected? As you have evolved and matured, has sex and sensuality been a part of you? Do you flirt and tease but never give in, knowing that you can use your sexual prowess as a source of power and control, keeping men drooling and buying your attention? Is this what you have been taught?

There are cultural mores that surround sex and intimacy. Be aware of your partner's views on sex and his definition of sex and relationship. Long into the relationship, is your partner still finding you attractive? Are you still willing to keep yourself attractive for your partner? As dating and then living together become more routine, has the togetherness revealed habits or personal behaviors that are now out there in the open? For example, when dating in the early stages, you met your partner after you had taken the time to do your hair, make up, and dress. Now, he sees you with bed head and blotchy skin. Is this the relationship that can withstand the bad hair days? Or is your partner particular, preferring to imagine you as one who wakes up with full makeup, as though he lives in a soap opera. You may need to test it out and come out of the shower with dripping hair and no foundation.

As for sex and intimacy, these are mutually exclusive and, then again, interchangeable. If sex has always been for fun and freedom, then share this with your partner. In centuries past, women and children were referred to as chattel. The sexual revolution has dramatically transitioned the role of women and equaled the playing field. You know it and everyone knows it, but have all populations of people embraced this? No, there is still the machismo in the veins of modern men. Do you feel equal to him when you and your partner engage in sexual activity? Are you expected to maintain your beauty and figure, while he can let himself go? Does he try to keep himself attractive and sexy to be pleasing to you? Are there times you feel objectified, beyond mutual agreement?

The Madonna-whore complex is real, and it applies to both men and women. This is when the man or woman craves the passion and desire of someone they do not see as "good." For example, a man who has this complex can see his girlfriend as a sexual partner, enjoying the erotic pleasure, but once this girlfriend becomes a wife and gives birth, the man soon loses his desire for her. This is a psychological problem that needs professional help. When a woman has this complex, she may appreciate the good and honorable man and accept being treated well, yet she desires the bad boy and then ultimately takes her good guy for granted. Being aware of sexual dysfunctions will alert you if something is amiss.

There was a time when men were not permitted in the delivery room. For men, this preserved their sexual perception by means of what they didn't see: the birth canal was what they only knew as the love canal. And because of this, their sex life was not altered—except for the fussy baby—which is another important reality for couples. When children come into the relationship, there is much joy; there are also fatigue and sleepless nights, and the love affair is now between baby and mama. Let's not neglect our man. He gets very sensitive when he starts to feel left out. The dads usually end up taking the back seat to this new love affair now known as motherhood. Nothing is wrong with devoting yourself to a needy infant, toddler, or child continuously. Luckily our hearts expand, which is why we can have more than one child. Our hearts remain with our man, too.

Generally, there are four types of sexual attractions we can play out, such as casual, romantic, familial, and erotic sex. If your relationship can maintain these with balance, you are in a very good place. Casual sex is meant to be part of spontaneous lovemaking. Outside a relationship and before a committed one, casual sex is what we will call "recreational," or like the kids call it today, "hooking up."

When emotions are involved and moods are not in sync, do you have the option to ask for a rain check in the bedroom, or does he sulk or make you feel guilty? Do you get accused of losing interest in him because your sex life has waned and two weeks have gone by since the last time you both had sex? Typically, the chemistry between the two of you is hot and heavy. For at least the first six months once the motor started running, each of you couldn't wait to rip each other's clothes off. Can that actually last? Has it lasted? If you have been together for more than two or three years, is it still hot and heavy? Much of this initial sexual chemistry is known as dopamine. This is the brain chemical that rushes through your body, and the brain triggers a need for more, like an addict strung out for his next fix.

Eventually, with other activities, new experiences, more involvement, and the need to get back to work on a normal schedule, less and less dopamine is being charged up to fuel the body. As the brain produces less, so the urge to produce more is reduced, and now the chemistry in the brain has responded to this chemical almost like in a detox, reducing its craving more and more. Sorry to say it, but much of the chemistry is part of our bigger design as a surviving species.

Men's and women's sex drives are very different. There are no exact rules, but communication is a vital component in your connection to your partner.

Without this chemistry, procreation would be in jeopardy, and human existence would be extinct. This, of course, is the layman's version of human biology. If you are interested in learning more about the science of sex, do your research.

As for the emotional side of sex, it's important to know that your committed relationship includes sex. Men's and women's sex drives are very different. There are no exact rules, but communication is a vital component in your connection to your partner when it comes to what is expected in the bedroom. What will the future look like as both of you age and engage? If you think your partner has an active libido, you should count on it staying that way. He is hoping your enjoyment of sex will remain a staple in your relationship, so pucker up. It's been stated that men have a sex cycle of 72 hours in general, which means after 72 hours without sex their brains start to quiver from withdrawal. This is not a clinical statement, but you can research it. This "theory" varies of course, but as you probably can attest, many men have admitted that they need sex, want sex, and have to have sex a lot more often than their female counterparts. Women find it challenging to keep up with this, almost placing a burden on us. Yet, 72 hours is a little less daunting than what we girls were told by boys, who said it was every 20 minutes that they had a sexual impulse or thought. Men also vary. Some men have been able to be comfortable with their sex drive; they continue to desire sex, but having developed sexual intelligence, they are better able to control this drive. By this I mean not making his partner feel guilty when she is not in the mood, or better yet, understanding that in order for his need to be met, he must develop an "appropriate" method to get her in the mood. "Appropriate" qualifies as respectful, perhaps tender, or romantic—that sort of thing—with the focus being on her.

This is a conversation you both should have together, if you haven't already. It may not be exactly clear or conclusive as to what the fair amount or frequency of sex for each of you may be in a given time, but getting a general baseline can help you both stay on the sex track without anyone feeling ignored, rejected, or misunderstood. When sex becomes taboo in the relationship or a topic that is uncomfortable to talk about, then you're in trouble. Seek professional help if things do not change. Waiting too long makes it more difficult to talk about it. When sex becomes an elephant in the room, the disconnect gets just as massive. I say: talk to a professional because talking about the intimacy of your relationship with a friend can attract more trouble. Personal issues such as these should remain personal; opening the window on something like this will also open the door and allow in a predator that neither of you want to contend with.

The sex and intimacy in the relationship should never be shortchanged. So JUST DO IT.

10 – Sex

Is there sex after marriage?

This is such a huge area of contention. Everyone is afraid to talk about it, and everyone has hang-ups. It is something you really don't know, but need to know, about the other person.

Women will hide who they really are when it comes to sex. Some will have sex only because they know the man likes it. Women have been learning since they were babies how to manipulate men. So while you were playing ball, riding bikes, and having fun, girls and then women were learning how to manipulate men to get things they needed by saying the things that needed to be said and behaving the way they needed to behave.

The difficult thing with some religions is they want you to be married before having sex. WHAT! How can you get married to someone and know your sex life will be great if you can't test this out before you get married? This just does not make sense to me. I also found along the way that some women will fake it until they make it, and I think you know what I mean. A lot of times, sex is used as a tool.

There are so many levels of sexual intelligence and intensities. Do you want to have sex once a year, once a week, once a day, or multiple times a day? Remember, when the kids come, sexual activity decreases. Ouch! So the very thing that got you to that point is not allowing you to do it anymore. Let's explore this topic and see how intelligent you are when it comes to sex. It's important to note that men need sex to be intimate, and women need intimacy in order to have sex. Before you say I do, you'd better know what's in her past, how she dealt with each of those situations, and the affect they had in her life.

It is a known fact that sex is a biological need for men. That is why you should take great care to choose a woman who has the same or similar appreciation for sex as you. That does not mean that you have to have sex multiple times a day or even once a day. Do what comes naturally, but make sure you are with a woman who is as sexual as you are. Most women need to feel emotionally connected in order for sex to be pleasurable. As a man, sex is an act that doesn't require an emotional connection, most of the time. Now that doesn't mean that sex isn't better with an emotional connection, because it can be great and not just a release.

> **It is a known fact that sex is a biological need for men. That is why you should take great care to choose a woman who has the same or similar appreciation for sex as you.**

If you are getting married, you want to make sure you have a very fulfilling sex life with your partner. It needs to be successful for both of you. If she is just performing her marital duties, it will never be the same as a lifelong appreciation of good sexual energy and intimacy. Know yourself: do you need mind-blowing sex all the time or are you OK with good sex most of the time? You may also change over time. Understand what you want and may need in the future, and know your partner's sexual wants and needs. It is important that both of you are honest with yourselves and each other and have many discussions on this topic. When you do not get your sexual needs met in a marriage, it carries over to the rest of your life. You may say to yourself, I could just masturbate and take care of myself. But believe me when I tell you, there is a difference. Masturbation does not give you the same connection with your partner, and it could also be a way of avoiding an issue between the two of you as well.

SEXUAL APPRECIATION LEVELS:

1. There are women who are perfectly fine not having sex for the rest of their lives or only having sex to procreate. Before marriage, they will have sex with you because they know you like it, but after they say, "I do," they may say, "I don't." They could be very deceiving, or they may not even know their motives, but be extremely sure you are not getting this type of woman, unless you hate sex yourself. Your life would most likely be miserable, or you may end up being unfaithful. Without sex, you may become angry, depression may set in, and you may withdraw and stop communicating. I'm not sure what kind of life this is for anyone, but the marriage reduces to one of existing together as two bodies in a house. There is very minimal love, if any at all, and neither of you really have any feelings towards each other. You have to look for the clues before you are married: she can only have sex when she is drunk or maybe she is only having sex when you do something for her.

2. The next level up is being with a woman who will have sex to perform her marital duties, but she is not having sex for her own pleasure or enjoyment. You will end

up doing your business, and there is no intimacy what-soever. This is one step above sex with an inanimate object or masturbation. This does not create a healthy marriage, and you will not be getting much out of this either, except for fulfilling a biological need. There will be similar clues as in the previous level, like she wants you to buy something for her and will have sex with you because you did something for her. Maybe she has a headache, or you are always pushing sex on her.

3. Next, you have a woman who enjoys sex to some degree but is not interested in trying new things. She probably would not give you oral sex and wants to just lay there in classic missionary style. There may be some intimacy and kissing, but she is not interested in doing any work during sex. You will know this type of woman because she is acting like this during the relationship and before marriage. She may give you oral sex, but she really doesn't like to. You have to look for the clues.

4. At the highest level, you will find a woman who likes sex and wants to explore and experiment with different things. This experimentation does not have to be at the level of a threesome or S&M. It is trying different posi-tions, maybe role-playing, etc. You can identify this type of woman because she will want to try different things before you are married. Also, look for the woman who will initiate sex. That is a huge clue.

OTHER THINGS TO THINK ABOUT:

•   Marriage never increases the sexual appetite, so if it is difficult to get her in the sack after you have started sexual activity, this will most likely get worse after marriage.

- Look for signs of conditional sex. She only has sex when you do something for her. I am not saying you don't have an obligation to get her in the mood, but she has to be willing to allow you to get her in the mood. If she completely dismisses you on occasion, that could be a very bad sign. Make sure you communicate what you are thinking, and see if the behavior changes or if she has good reasons.

- Make sure you talk about sex, or when you are having sex, see what turns her on and learn about her. Does she like dirty talk? You need to know these things about her to help you get what you want. It is a two-way street. You want her to stay interested and not dread sex.

- Understand her values about sex. Did her family openly discuss sex; were they afraid to talk about it? Is sex a dirty word or does she love talking about it, texting about it, etc.?

- Does she like to be private, does she like the lights off, or does everything have to be perfect before she is in the mood?

- Sexual hang-ups may include things from her past. Make sure you know if there was any sexual trauma, such as rape or molestation. This will definitely affect her thinking about sex.

- You need to understand your own sexual hang-ups. Are you honest with yourself and not just being the macho man? Understand what really works for you. Absolutely do not get into a heterosexual marriage if you are having doubts about your sexuality. It will only be worse later, and you will bring your partner a lot of pain.

- Has your partner been sexually educated at school, on the street, by family and friends? Understand what she knows, what she is comfortable doing, and what her boundaries are. You may find that oral sex is a boundary but that it may happen once a year as a birthday present.

As men, we need sex. It's not an option. Sex is an important part of our lives. Taking sex away from us can make us completely different people. If you have not had sex in a long time, then think about how different you may have become. Be aware of the changes in your demeanor on a daily basis. As a man, you need to be fulfilled in this area, just as women need to be fulfilled emotionally in their lives. So make sure you are with someone who will provide for you, and in return, you need to provide for her.

11 – Money

Do you see dollar signs when you look into his eyes?

This topic needs special attention. Money is a major source of conflict in a relationship. At the very beginning of dating, usually the value of money becomes apparent, or else remains hidden and not easily traceable. Pay attention, and if it's not clear, talk about it. It's another elephant that you do not want in your room.

As women, we have been conditioned when we accept a date to expect the man to pay. Most women would admit that it is typical for the man to ask for the check at the restaurant and, without hesitancy, pull out his wallet and throw down bills or his American Express card. On the second date, he wants to impress you with another evening out, possibly including a meal or an event, but again would throw down the money or whip out his credit card without batting an eye. Let's recall that, by the second date, it's clear you are enjoying each other and a third date is very likely. Now what? He has shown an interest and in his mind has made an investment by doling out the cash. Should he expect some reciprocity by now? By this time, women hold various feelings when it comes to the fork in the dating road.

Money is a major source of conflict in a relationship.

Maybe you recognize yourself in one of the following four personalities:

1. There are women who feel that reciprocity includes sex. Is it because the man who has been paying for her company now expects a return? For the applicable woman, this is a result of conditioning, and it may become the expected response when the man has dropped a few hints and compliments, if she hasn't been groomed to thank him with a mere "thank you;" instead she responds with sexual favors or feels obligated to return the gesture in other creative ways. This sets the tone for a conditional relationship, similar to the dynamic within her family of origin, which taught her that you didn't get something for nothing.

2. The second type is the woman who continues to allow the man to pay, never once offering or even thinking to offer to do so, and who believes that it would be improper for him to expect her to consider the thought. There is no conditional reciprocity here at all. She feels he enjoys her company and therefore is willing to pay for it, with no obligation on her part.

3. The insightful, mature woman will exhibit a mutual liking and therefore offer to take him out. This is a relationship revolving around fairness, honesty, and individuality.

4. The fourth personality type is none of the above. She may have grown up with money, and money was never a basis for conditions—merely a tool. It has always been there, not necessarily in her pocketbook, but perhaps her parents or grandparents supported her. Someone else always picks up the check, not her.

There are many personality variations based on many factors, but these four personalities are the most traditional scenarios. Many of these values depend on how you were raised or how you learned to think about money. The way you respond consciously in a relationship when money and finances are involved will most likely form the basis of the relationship. However, for many unfortunates who end up in bitter divorces, the biggest battle is about MONEY, which becomes a metaphor for much of what is wrong between the two parties. Money battles during the divorce tap into deep-seated fear and power. Interestingly, there is a fine line between the two.

What is money for you? Is it an extension of your identity, or perhaps a status symbol, or a tool to be used for maintaining a lifestyle? Is there anxiety about money? Do you consider yourself a spender, a saver, austere, fearless, or entitled? Were you taught the value of a dollar, or did you grow up not worrying about where the next dollar was coming from? Was it always plentiful in your home of origin, and did your parents bankroll all your needs and wants? Or were you taught to sacrifice for it? Did you get an allowance and have to work, tending to chores in order to receive a stipend to be spent any way you wished? Did you come from a family, perhaps a single-parent household, where money was carefully budgeted, and in order to have certain luxuries or even necessities, you or your parent(s) needed to save? Or were there mixed messages between both parents?

There are various values around money, and one is not better or worse than the other. A value is a value, but regardless of your value about money, you and your partner must talk about it. He will need to share with you his value around money. Asking your partner how he views money will reveal information you both need to know. When a couple views money the same way or differently, the dynamic in the relationship will either be nonconflictual or conflictual, respectively. If your values around money are as far apart as the North and South Poles, you both could find yourselves in money struggles. Money values that are not respected will churn internal turmoil. When money values are dishonored and thereby affect your relationship, symptoms will emerge and plague it. It's possible that you both could develop a new set of values around money in order to avoid big pitfalls. But the truth is, values are tough to alter. The best solution is not to lose sight of your different values, and if it means having separate bank accounts later on and a financial planner, then it's worth it. Values are formed in the early years, beginning with the family of origin, and it's very difficult to change someone else's belief system.

Asking your partner how he views money will reveal information you both need to know. Money values that are not respected will churn internal turmoil.

The most important scenario of all is if you are in a relationship with someone who spends and gathers debt without ever losing sleep. Don't think you are going to improve your financial future by paying it off for him or her. You will only be frustrated when he or she racks up more debt. Don't be fooled by the promises from your loved one that they are going to change any time soon.

Money values can be seen in many ways, but it helps to talk about your views on money. People often shy away from discussing topics such as money. IT'S OK to TALK ABOUT MONEY. Ask your partner a simple question: if they were gifted a huge sum of money, what would they do with it? Use a number that is relevant to them, for a gift of $1,000.00 could be a lot to one person, as much as $100,000.00 to another. So to get a fair assessment, approximate a close sum. Your partner might give one of the following general responses: spend all of it until it's gone, enjoying the extravagance; spend a portion and save a portion (you might want to ask what sizes the portions are); or use it to pay off debt. Perhaps another idea is in their mind, but whatever it is, make sure they are not saying it to either impress you or impress themselves.

Your partner may come from money, or come from poverty. This of course does not necessarily mean they are of a wealthy or an impoverished mind-set. In fact, their family and experience may have made an impact and triggered in them the opposite of what they lived.

If your partner grew up with wealth or means, such that whatever they wanted was there for the asking, then growing up with all the latest fashions and electronics taught them that if they wanted something—poof—it appeared. To them, money was plentiful and never in a state of drought. Or perhaps they grew up affluent but were raised to earn what they wanted. So if money was available, great, but they learned the value of that allowance, and when it was spent, it meant working to earn more.

Then, there's the partner's family who did not exactly have money, yet felt the tug of guilt when they couldn't indulge. Instead, they borrowed, went into debt, and sacrificed in order to keep up with the other families. Whoever grows up in this type of household has been kept in the dark, sheltered from reality. "When you don't have it, spend it anyway and worry about it later." There is also the belief that "if you raise the bar higher than your current income, it will force you to earn more." Admirable, yet risky. The one thing to watch out for is the partner who is dazzled by all the goods they see. Are they a sucker for a brand-name item? Is quality compromised for label? Do they buy the best, eat the best, and drive the best because they can afford it and deserve it, or deserve it without being able to afford it?

When you travel with your partner, what are the accommodations like? Are you both in agreement on how to vacation? Do you both want to spend it all and go wild with five-star everything: hotel, restaurants, front-row seats, first-class tickets, express line, and new wardrobe just for the trip? Granted, if you're dating a tycoon or a sheik, then money is flowing like oil. But for the majority of the human population in the volatile economy, we must maintain control over our financial responsibilities. And the best way to do that if you choose to be in a relationship and join financials is to address the money values immediately and take them seriously. Remember, you have been warned. IT'S OK to TALK ABOUT THE MONEY.

Besides sex, kids, and in-laws, money is the make-or-break reality of any relationship. In the end, the biggest dispute, other than the kids, is—you've got it—the money.

Money can also act as a metaphor for deeper issues in a relationship. Yet those deeper issues rarely get discovered because money is such a large entity and its tentacles reach around so many other issues, squeezing the life out of all it wraps around.

The easiest way to find out if you and your partner will go bankrupt, live wealthily, or be steadily comfortable is to talk about it. What is important to you, what is important for your partner, and how do both of you respect the value of money?

12 – Money

Does she mistake your initials for ATM?

The subject of money values is not just about the state of having money. It is also about how you spend money. What are your money values? How does money affect you? What were your parents like with money? How much money did you have growing up? Etcetera. This is at the core of your money values. Just to give you an example, someone may feel that unless you have 100 presents under the Christmas tree, it is not Christmas. That is an exaggeration, but you get the idea. You may also find someone who is not interested in saving money, but wants to spend every penny; they don't worry about where the money will come from later and live paycheck to paycheck. Some people want to take their money, save as much as they can, and invest in stocks, bonds, real estate, etc. Some are very careful with money and would shop wisely to get value, purchase goods at a good price, and always use coupons. The point I want to make is that most marriages fail because of money.

Read through the following different dating scenarios now and in the future.

MONEY VALUES REFLECTED IN DATING SITUATIONS

1. **Dating Situation #1:**

   Do you feel that every time a bill or check comes or you are put in a position to pay, you are always reaching into your pocket, but your date is not? Do you feel better about yourself when you pay for everything? Does that make you feel like a real man?

   The good and the bad:

   Right now while dating, if you are making good money and you are paying for everything, then you may feel like you are on top of the world. You feel like a real man and are OK with things the way they are. You know you can make money, you have never had a problem making money, and you are very resourceful. Remember, this may be the case now, but you are putting yourself in a very vulnerable position. She has been conditioned to believe that men should always pay her way. This is a very dangerous woman when it comes to money. In the marriage, she will make up any excuse not to work, and she will continue to have babies just to avoid going to work. The children will be in high school, and she will still have a reason for needing to be with the kids, to be there for them, JUST IN CASE! In any future divorce, this type of woman will take you to the cleaners. You have set her up to think that you should pay her way, so don't think that will stop when you divorce. She will not stop and will not be happy until she has every penny of yours. The courts look favorably on these types of women and feel you should continue to pay her way. Some men have even been burdened with paying maintenance (alimony) for life for her type. Don't let anyone tell you this does not happen anymore, because it does happen if you have the right, or in this case the wrong, judge.

2. **Dating Situation #2:**

When you are out on a date, the woman makes an effort to pay for some of the check. She doesn't share evenly with everything, but she makes an effort and does not immediately assume you are paying for everything.

The good and the bad:

This type of woman may be the one that works part-time; she always had a job, but never had a career. Pay close attention to this because you may have the woman who also would take you to the cleaners, but may not push as hard or expect as much as the woman in the previous Situation #1.

3. **Dating Situation #3:**

When you are out on a date, the woman needs to share in every dinner and expense that you incur. She never assumes you are paying for everything and doesn't feel comfortable with you paying for everything.

The good and the bad:

This type of woman has a career. She may love her job or hate it. However, she is not expecting all the money to come from you. She will be fair with everything. She probably works full-time and may even love her job. That's a great thing. Be happy with this. You don't have to be the moneyman. In a divorce, this woman will not take you to the cleaners. She will not feel comfortable asking the courts for you to pay her maintenance.

4. **Dating Situation #4:**

This woman pays for everything. Maybe she knows you don't have as much money as she, and she has plenty.

Either she makes a lot of money or she has money in her family. At some point she may feel like you are a loser, or she may just enjoy the fact that she has more money than you. This may feel very emasculating for you. Understand your feelings and be honest. It may feel good now, but it may wear thin eventually. Know yourself; don't just think it couldn't be wrong to accept this. It may not matter as much now but could eventually matter a lot. You need to be sure how you are feeling. Don't be in denial, only to hurt both of you later.

The good and the bad:

In a divorce, you will ABSOLUTELY NOT be taken to the cleaners. She has always enjoyed paying for you. You may even end up getting maintenance from her. Also remember, if this woman was born into money and she has a rich daddy, the daddy may come after you with a vengeance. If there are kids involved, you will probably lose custody because you won't have enough money to fight off her lawyer. You will lose because you just don't have the money to keep fighting.

SPENDER VERSUS SAVER

Another way to look at money values is to see who is the spender and who is the saver. If you are preparing to combine your money, you should know what type you are marrying or have married.

1. **Spender with a woman who likes to save:**
   If you are a spender, then you will be OK spending, but your future wife may not be, and you may really hate keeping your spending to a minimum. You will think that she is stingy and a penny-pincher. She may always

be asking you where your money is going, and you will have to justify your expenses. She may also stop you from spending on something you really want. This will definitely not feel good for you. You will need to work hard in the relationship to curb your spending and to change your sense of entitlement. The day when you do not have enough money to buy the things you wish will be the day you are unhappy, and that will carry over into the relationship.

2. **Spender with a woman who likes to spend:**
    In this relationship, you'd better never get married, and you should continue to live with your parents. You will continue to spend more money than you have and will live paycheck to paycheck. You could never retire unless you are waiting for your inheritance to do so. You should recognize that because both of you like to spend and may feel a sense of entitlement to spending on nice things, as soon as the money dries up, you will both be struggling in the relationship. Both of you will be miserable, and it will definitely affect the relationship and most likely end up in divorce unless you are able to really work hard to change your thinking about money and recognize that it's where the unhappiness starts.

3. **Saver with a woman who likes to spend:**
    If you are a saver and you have a woman who likes to spend, you will not be happy with her spending habits. You will think she is irresponsible with money, and it will feel like she is impulsive. She wants to live in the present and enjoy the money that is available now. Every month, you will be unhappy with the credit card bills, and you will want her to explain where all the

money went. She will rationalize everything she spent, but you still will not be happy with so much money going out, especially if you want to save for the future. This type of person may run up a credit card bill that cannot be paid back for several years. As a saver, this will completely frustrate you. You need to be aware if she has Gucci bags and $3,000 shoes. If these were purchased by her with her money, that's great. But if they were purchased by someone else, BEWARE! Even if you keep your money separate in the marriage, when the day comes that she does not have the money to buy the things she wants, she will not be happy and the relationship will suffer. It will take a lot of work on her part to change this type of thinking.

4. **Saver with a woman who likes to save:**
    In this relationship, it could work out really well. You will never be trying to keep up with the Joneses, but you will have plenty of money for retirement. Both of you like to save, and you are not impulsive spenders. You will overthink and analyze every buying decision, even a small purchase. You are both very responsible people, but you will look like the squeakiest couple in the neighborhood. In addition, when you go out to dinner with people, you will need to get a separate check because you never go all out when at dinner or on a vacation, even if you win the lottery. You will hate splitting the bill with people because they got three entrees, four appetizers, drank themselves into oblivion, and topped it off with a nice dessert or two and a double espresso with amaretto.

As you can see, there are many different flavors, and knowing what you will have to deal with before it happens goes a long way. Every couple has money issues at some time in the relationship. Knowing the way you and your partner handle money will alleviate a lot of pain and suffering. The "love" of money may be the root of all evil, but evil things happen when you don't have enough of it.

♀ – DANA

13 –Compatibility

Do you really know him?

Would you say that compatibility plays a significant role in a stable relationship? Most women would say absolutely it does. The rest who do not see it as significant may be in the relationship for another reason, and if that is the case with you, you need to go back and read the chapter on examining your motivation to marry so that the wedding bells you hear ring are not just the ringing in your head. This word, compatibility, gets thrown around a lot when it comes to dating and meeting someone new. We usually refer to it as meaning having things in common. I have often checked with couples on what they share as a common interest, and I get answers such as "We like the same band," or "We both like to sleep in on Sundays." "OK", I say, "what else?" The room gets silent.

The essence of compatibility is important, and most couples would agree that if they had not met the basic level of compatibility, they couldn't possibly have

Compatibility plays a significant role in a stable relationship and should not be confused with sexual chemistry. Great sex is vital to the intimacy of the relationship, but it shouldn't define it.

gotten past the third date.

Compatibility should not be confused with sexual chemistry, and if you think because the sex is out of the universe that this makes for compatibility, sorry, no score here. Great sex is vital to the intimacy of the relationship, but it shouldn't define it.

I believe, based on the many couples I have worked with over the years, that compatibility is the ability to complement each other's sensibility. Take these two ideas—complement and ability—and combine them into companionship. Companionship includes temperament, values, ambition, mental state, and interests that advance or inspire us. Even though compatibility may appear to mean that you share the same interests, this is not always the case.

Compatibility can mean having different interests while enjoying an interest in each other's interest, without having to take on that interest and make it one of your own. See, the beauty in this is that you may appreciate your partner's interests without having to be a part of them. For example, he loves to watch sports on TV; you don't, but you can enjoy his enjoyment in it.

Another way of being truly compatible is when both of you can sit across from each other while eating a bowl of soup and be content with each other's company, just enjoying the soup. Silence throughout the eating of the soup is nice, and perhaps before or after the soup, you have shared an exchange of thoughts and ideas. This exchange excludes gossip, complaints, or criticisms of any kind. There's one brief quote I'd like to mention at this point. I read this inside my kitchen cabinet back in the 1960s (where my wise mother had taped a bunch of quotes and sayings) that must have been from Ann Landers: "Small people talk about other people, average people talk about things, and intelligent people talk about ideas." Keeping that in mind may help focus a conversation. The other tidbit of wisdom I received was from my brother in the 1970s when I started dating. He said, "Dana, whatever happens and whoever you become, just don't be a bitch." My brother did not tape that up in the kitchen cabinet, he said it right to my face as I ran out the door to meet my boyfriend at the time. Have I developed my own philosophical outlook? Yes, and so shall you.

Consider compatibility with your companion as that same wonderful feeling you had when you were young: sharing a time with your best friend, laughing, crying, confessing hopes and dreams; or the closeness you felt with family. If for some reason you or your partner is missing this feeling, then reconsider your situation. Companionship and compatibility are what draw you to want to share your life with your partner. It is that feeling that you don't get with anyone else, and it always leaves you wanting more. Companionship and compatibility are also the feelings you get that cause you to desire more for your partner. You are genuinely interested in what he has to say, what he likes to do, and what he is feeling about particular areas and interests in his life. Even though those interests do not appeal to you, the appreciation that he is interested is enough for you. If he has a hobby or goes to join his friends at the gym or racetrack, you understand his enthusiasm. You are, for the most part, in sync with his interest, as he is in sync with yours. Sharing the pleasure, both collectively and individually, allows an equal balance of life's joys.

As you and your partner move through life, the interests you once shared may come to no longer exist. You both may have developed new interests due to lifestyle or physical changes; or maybe something new came along and took priority over the previous one. There are many reasons why interests can change over time. Compatibility in the relationship should remain, regardless. Both of you will encourage each other to venture out to expand yourselves, continually adding new layers to your life, keeping your lives interesting with inner growth, and maintaining a skill or learning new ones.

♂ – DON

14 – Compatibility

Do you really know her?

Everyone has their own idea of what makes two people compatible in a relationship or marriage. The idea is to find out what's right for you. You could be happy having the traditional Husband and Wife roles; you could be happy seeing your partner only on the weekends. The important thing to remember is that as long as the needs of you and your partner are being met, that's what matters. What happens all too often is that people get married without fully understanding what they are getting into because they love their partner today. But what they don't take into account are the things that may cause the marriage to fail in the future. In order for you to really understand your partner, you must understand yourself and start the process of being curious about you and your partner.

It is extremely difficult today to get married when you are just out of high school or still in college. You feel at that time that things are so great, you know everything you need to know, and you feel so happy with the person you picked. Our minds are still developing well into our twenties. Don't you think that might make a difference when you are 26 years old? If you get married before the age of 26, things may change later when it develops. Do some research on brain development in your twenties and see how things could change for you.

However, just realize you may be fooling yourself and your partner. You have not even had the chance to live alone without your parents. The only way to understand you is to put yourself in different situations that will make you aware of how you behave and how you feel about things that you do, say, and feel. In addition, have you had one relationship or have you had many? How do you feel about each one

> **Use the Questionnaire section at the end of this book as a tool to initiate discussions and become more aware of aspects about you and your partner.**

of those relationships? Each one can teach you things about yourself, about your partner, and about your future partners, if any. Understanding your partner in a new, deep way is the key to a better, more fruitful marriage. Please go to the Questionnaire section at the end of the book, to get a list of questions that will help make you aware of aspects about you and your partner. Some will matter more than others, but discussing them with your partner and using them as a tool to get the discussions going will help tremendously.

SIGNS OF TROUBLE

Be aware of the things that bother you now that you used to think were cute or OK.

- Things that annoy you, such as:
  – When the toilet paper is put in the wrong way.
  – The glasses are down instead of up or vice versa.
  – The towels or laundry are not folded right.
- Texting when at dinner
- Partner stares at other people consistently

- No real affection most of the time
- Sex has gone from once a week to once a month, once every two months, or is non-existence.
- You are arguing a lot
- One or both of you criticize the other on a regular basis.
- One of you is giving the other the cold shoulder or are just annoyed when that person speaks.
- Your partner is always undermining you, or telling you how great she is, or how bad you are compared to her.

There are a lot of things to consider and think about when you are in a relationship. Every relationship has its problems, but can you weather the storm? More importantly, have you picked a woman who can weather the storm, or will she pick up and go at the first sign of trouble? The choice is yours, and don't think a divorce will make your problems go away. When there is a child involved and you picked the wrong woman, you just might as well kiss your ass goodbye because you will live in agony the rest of your life. She will alienate you from the children and give you hell every chance she can. Of course if you pick the right woman, divorce can be mediated, and life can be amicable after a divorce. Even better, pick someone with whom you can grow and develop, be a best friend, and be partners during the good and the bad times. Whom do you have?

15 –Communication

Can he talk the talk?

If you read any chapter over again, this one should be it. When you are interacting with any one person or group of people, strangers or those familiar, friends or family, what is it that you do? Communicate. I know you know that. So why are there arguments, misunderstandings, and feuds that end relationships? Communication gone wrong is the answer.

As for you and your partner, communication is the key to success. Communication is not only expressing what you think or feel. Many of the arguments in relationships come down to what isn't being expressed. Often times one partner feels the other is not communicating at all. So one would think, however, that the non-communicator is expressing quite a bit within their silence. For the partner who feels shut out, this can turn into a battle cry.

Verbal communication is the key to success. Silence can shut out the partner and turn to a battle cry.

Think about a time when you and your partner were getting along beautifully. Now think of a time when you weren't. Why was that? What happened? Was something said that shouldn't have been said? Was something NOT said that should have been said? Was something said, but misinterpreted, and one of you felt hurt or angry?

Are there times when you and your partner do not address an issue that is a sensitive topic, and when it gets avoided, feelings are still ruminating? Is it fair to say that broaching a subject that hits a nerve within either one of you is avoided mostly because one or both of you are fearful of the discussion escalating to an unpleasant argument? It doesn't have to be a debate or an argument that will either ruin the moment, ruin the day, or ruin the relationship. That is so sad and so unhealthy, so unnecessary. If this is the concern, then folks, your relationship has big problems in the communication arena.

A relationship that develops and grows on a healthy foundation includes communicating on all topics, pleasant and unpleasant.

A relationship that develops and grows on a healthy foundation includes communicating on all topics, pleasant and unpleasant.

Think about a sensitive issue that one or both of you find uncomfortable. For example, a hot-button topic could be an ex-girlfriend who is still contacting your boyfriend and she isn't being discreet about it. The bigger problem is that he is not standing up to her and telling her that he is in a serious relationship, or saying anything that discourages her from contacting him. You explain to your boyfriend that you don't like this girl thinking it's OK to flirt with him, and you want him to tell her to stop calling, texting, e-mailing or whatever. Your boyfriend doesn't see the harm. He is not interested in her, doesn't find her a threat, and believes the problem lies within you. All you are asking is for him to respect you by telling her to back off and hit the road.

Secretly, you think he likes the attention and won't do anything immediately to stop it. This infuriates you, and the more you feel dismissed, the angrier you become. Every time the subject comes up, words are communicated. If it escalates to an argument, then it's apparent that the leverage and equality is off-kilter. In other words, an argument arises when one feels they are not getting what they want or need and attempts to win it for themselves. When it is a debate and a negotiation, it is not about power and control or necessarily winning or losing. Be aware of how communication is expressed and conflicts are resolved and the difference between an argument and a negotiation. A healthy, balanced relationship involves both individuals either obtaining what it is they need, and when that is not possible, it entails a fair compromise.

An argument ensues when one side does not feel equal to the other side. If both sides feel they are being equally heard and honored–poof!–no argument. The trick is to master that concept. Until then, in order for both sides to feel equal, the communication needs to be expressed equally. The best way is to speak from "I." Too often we argue with "blame" and a "YOU did this to ME" attack. When we communicate, it is best practice to use the "I get hurt or annoyed (or whatever the applicable feeling) when I'm feeling disrespected" approach. This concept is known as Speaker/Listener. The ideal way to communicate when defensiveness gets triggered is to stick with "I" statements. Each needs to listen to the other speak and not be preoccupied with what you're going to say next. If you speak over each other, no one is really hearing the other.

If both sides feel they are being equally heard and honored–poof!–no argument.

If this is the case, then each needs to repeat back what the other said. Take turns in speaking, even if you have to use a "talking stick," which I call any object that the speaker holds to maintain permission to speak without being interrupted; this is also a good practice for self-control. Usually in a heated argument, both parties feel they need to rush their words to get their point across, although it never works because neither one is listening. It's exhausting and unproductive.

Body language and expressions tell more about a person than the words that come out of their mouth. Study your fella. Know what his body is saying to you. What is the expression on his face saying? Does he get quiet when he is pre-occupied with work, or does he problem solve in his head rather than talk it out? Generally, women are talkers and problem solve as they speak. Men tend to problem solve in their heads, and then talk once it is resolved. Find out if you or your partner fit into either category. Know how each of you operates when it comes to problem solving, concerns, planning, and tasking. When are you most communicative?

If you have not been communicating about what matters to each of you, then that had better be all you are doing from this point on— communicating, that is.

Does each of you talk about your dreams, silly thoughts, and serious ideas? Does each of you feel safe and unjudged by the other when speaking freely about personal matters? Can either of you express to the other without the fear that it will be misinterpreted, dismissed, or criticized?

The most important thing is this: if you have not been communicating about what matters to each of you, then that had better be all you are doing from this point on—

communicating, that is. Without communication you have nothing. Without communication you can only guess what each is saying, and you have a 50% chance of being right. Not good odds. Another big mistake is that couples assume they know their partners. Jumping to conclusions is never a good idea, no matter how many years you know each other. When doing this, you may think you know your guy, but you really aren't in his head. Some take offense at the assumption that their partner knows what they think and what they feel. Some are flattered that their partner knows them so well and can speak for them because they have been tuned in. This is something else you both can talk about.

Couples think it's silly to talk about talking. Those who think it's silly are the ones who will argue more and more down the road, if their relationship even lasts. Sorry, I'm just saying it like it is. Of course there are those couples who say they never argue. It's very possible, as long as no one is holding back, avoiding an argument. Healthy arguing and expressing your thoughts, feelings, beliefs, convictions, wants, and needs is what being in a relationship is all about. If you are in a committed, exclusive relationship, then it's essential, and it deepens the intimacy. Open, honest communication is the key to a successful relationship.

There is always more to learn about each other. When you find yourselves with quality time to talk, try adding to the conversation thought-provoking questions about moral issues, political positions, values, and questions about family of origin. The art of conversation runs deep. If you practice this, you will never be at a loss for good talks. If you see a movie or have a meal, talk about it, critique it, and share with each other your impressions. Having a critical eye or a sophisticated palate will stimulate conversation and take it further than, "I liked it." Don't settle. Raise your consciousness about areas that you have wondered about but never disciplined yourself to learn more about. Asking questions that get your partner talking about a topic he likes will stimulate the conversation. A little-known fact is that most people love to talk about themselves. Asking questions in regard to your partner's interests will get the conversation going. Showing your interest, without stating a negative opinion, but rather offering more positive and encouraging feedback, can really keep the conversation flowing.

Here's one more important factor to consider: if you and your partner tend to interrupt each other when you both speak, one or both of you are probably annoyed. Be considerate and try not to overpower the conversation. Which one of you has to get your point across first? There's plenty of time to share your thoughts and feelings; conversation is not a race to the finish line. I encourage you to take this advice and experiment. The relationship will become stale if the connection remains limited.

♂ – DON

16 – Communication

Does she talk way too much?

Communication is the single thing that can make or break any relationship. From a man's perspective, women talk way too much. Remember men, all women think we never communicate enough. Women are wondering, "Where did he go; why does he not say what he feels; and what do I need to do to get him to talk, etc."

There are different levels of communication:

- **Broadcast** – You talk to your partner and either don't wait for a response or don't even listen to a response. You have been heard by her, and that's all that matters. The only issue with this is that you may not have been heard at all.
- **Single Channel** – You talk to your partner and listen to what she says but don't really hear her or make sure you know what she means. You heard what she said, and you believe you know what she meant. The issue with this is that she may have said one thing and meant something totally different.
- **Dual Channel** – You talk to your partner and listen to what she says. You then take the time to repeat back to her what you heard and make sure that you understand what she meant.

• **Fully Engaged** – You talk to your partner, listen to what she says, repeat back what you think she said, watch her body language, and then make sure her behavior matches what she says.

Are you taking the time to improve your communication skills in your relationship? Do you even care? You'd better care because better communication makes her happy or, at a minimum, allows you to be aware of her unhappiness before a divorce is initiated. Also, if women know that they are being heard, they will generally be happier. It still may not save you from a divorce or reduce the number of sexless days, but you definitely have a better shot at saving the marriage, increasing your happiness, increasing the happiness of the whole family, and last but not least, increasing your chances of having sex more often.

As I stated before, communication, or the lack of it, can have serious effects on the relationship. For instance, if you are having some money issues or you lose your job and are feeling like crap, if you don't express how you are feeling, it will eat at you daily and will definitely affect your relationship. However, if you discuss how you are feeling with your partner and let her know how bad things are, you have a much better shot at helping her understand. You may be saying to yourself that you don't have to tell her because "How could she not know how I feel." Well, you need to tell her anyway, and you need to tell her every day because she may not know. By communicating to her everything you are feeling, you make sure she is aware. You should also make an effort to understand how she is feeling and don't just listen to her words. Make sure you understand what her words mean to her!

There are also a lot of men who will listen to what their partners are saying, taking it all in. However, men have a tendency to analyze instead of communicating right away how they feel. Men are not used to talking about their feelings, and when they hear something from their partner, they may just go "cerebral." Going cerebral means their brains immediately start working on what they heard. They may continue to do this analysis work for two or three more days and then discuss it with their partner after they have thought about it. Just remember, women do not process this way. They usually talk and react to what they have heard. Therefore, if you want to make your partner happy, tell her exactly what you thought you heard. You may be overthinking something for two or three days, and you may be completely off base. She may have meant something completely different than what you thought she said. Get in the habit of repeating what you thought she said and then listening to what she says afterward. Never accuse or blame her, but tell her about what you feel. Always start off the sentence with "I feel you are," and never start with "You are doing." If she says you are blaming her or accusing her, remind her, "This is how YOU are feeling."

Trust me, the more you talk and the more you really understand what she is feeling and saying, the stronger your relationship will be.

Make communication a priority and make improving your communication skills a priority. The more opportunities you have to learn about how your partner communicates, the better. Trust me, the more you talk and the more you really understand what she is feeling and saying, the stronger your relationship will be. You should continue to strive to the "Fully Engaged Level," and don't even stop there. Make sure her behavior follows what she is saying, and call her out on things that don't match up. Don't stop until it makes sense to you. You owe it to yourself and your partner to understand her completely.

♀ – DANA

17 –Cohabitation

Have you really given this serious thought?

Depending on your personality style and your comfort zone, deciding to live together can be a joint enhancement to both your lives. If there are idiosyncrasies that are noticeable, it's best to talk about them. Also, it's a fact that we humans carry neuroses with us. A neurosis is not always a cause for a mental health assessment. In its basic definition, a neurosis is an unfulfilled need that occurs in infancy and from then on expresses itself as an anxiety to meet that need. It sounds worse than it is. However, some individuals have severe forms of neuroses. You yourself or your partner may have them, and if they're being addressed, good. This acceptance of an unfulfilled need in your partner is going to be a very crucial factor when life together becomes a bit unraveling. And it most likely will. Your jobs are to uncover what that unfulfilled need is. Without shame or criticism. *(I just needed to throw that in.)*

Making the decision to live together sometimes has more to do with economics. Often couples decide to combine their finances in order to save money and plan for a better financial future. Combining finances allows for money to be saved and, in turn, allows for more resources. Couples who have lived separately come to the realization that having two separate homes no longer makes sense if they are together every night or almost every night. For couples who choose to combine their resources and try living together before marriage, it is a sure way to discover more about their partner. But there needs to be an exit plan, just in case it doesn't work out. Having exit plans in place can save the relationship or prevent each of you from making a mistake that is irreversible.

Living together can be a joint enhancement to both your lives. There needs to be commitment as well as an exit plan, just in case it doesn't work out.

For couples who like the way things are and for whom the arrangement of living separately works, there are many benefits to this as well. Living apart may not save money but may save other priorities, like personal space. In later-life relationships, perhaps after numerous long-term ones or failed marriages, those who have previously lived with another or were divorced may not be so eager to live together in their current relationship. They have experienced this already and now choose a different path. That's not to say it has anything to do with living together, per se.

Cohabitation is a commitment. It requires a dialogue regarding the roles, tasks, and shared responsibilities. It also must factor in lifestyle, temperament, routine, personal preferences, and joint preferences. Money is now a major matter in the cohabitation. Who is paying for what? Does one make more income? Does the other have a parent who provides extras? What shared expenses are paid out of whose bank account? What if one loses their job—does the other carry them? These logistical details are important, of course. Money values are highlighted in this living situation.

Traditional habits may be hard to break. While dating and going out socially or away on vacation, when the two of you planned and shared expenses, were those shared expenses discussed? Had there been a change over time with the distribution of expenses? In the earlier part of your relationship was one most often paying the tabs? Has this been the norm and will this change or stay the same? Since you are not married, income is not a marital asset. When two people live together unmarried and then break up, money accrued is not divided up. Therefore, whatever money was spent on trips, furniture, groceries, etc. is not accounted for. Is there one of you who is generous just by choice? If the union divides, each takes their belongings and goes. There is no credit for appliances bought or purchases made. If either or both have ever been married before, they know that the difference between unmarried cohabitation and marriage is that marriage is a legal contract, broken only by the letter of the law, and living together is not.

Living together can lead to a legal contract. Should that be the future plan? Living together will certainly give you the insight that you both need as to where the areas of conflict lie. Conflicts will emerge, and living together will undoubtedly challenge you both. The key is to create your couple-hood consciously instead of the couple-hood creating you. Make the conscious effort to be deliberate in cultivating the relationship in the way you both want it to take shape and

Cultivate the relationship in the way you both want it to take shape and develop. Every successful business has a business plan. Just because it's romantic and love is the core motive, don't overlook the benefits of conscious cocreation.

develop. Many couples miss this very important component. Every successful business has a business plan. Just because it's romantic and love is the core motive, don't overlook the benefits of conscious cocreation. Both of you can get a lot more traction and fulfillment by planning and talking about every single thing. Don't hesitate just because you think it's petty minutia.

It has been said many times and for years that relationships have ended over toothpaste. And you should believe it. If you have ever lived with anyone before or shared a room with your sibling, you know. The slightest annoyance can drive you up the wall—not just annoyed, but turned off. Of course, by now you know who snores the loudest and which one of you sleeps the latest, which means the earlier riser walks the dog or makes the coffee. But which one of you leaves the dishes in the sink until the morning, or if they have a cold, leaves the chore they agreed is theirs to wait until their immune system is fully functioning? How about the preference for spring cleaning? If one of you has strict beliefs and rituals around the annual spring purge—window washing; curtains and blinds; transitioning closets from winter clothes to spring and summer wardrobes; putting boots, gloves, ski equipment away—while the other thinks "what a waste of a good weekend," does this mean spring cleaning gets support and team effort? It's very difficult to induct someone into a household chore that they never knew anything about, never watched their parent doing when growing up, or never have any

You should believe the old saying that relationships have ended over toothpaste. Being aware of personal preferences will save a lot of frustration later on.

intention of participating in though they can see the point of it. Maybe during the early years there is an interest and some assistance, but if it's not heartfelt, I guarantee it's going to end up a solo endeavor. Learning the habits of each other can and usually will be quite an eye-opening experience, though manners are observed to some extent at the beginning.

Don't be too impressed if your Mr. Yard Work opts for mowing the lawn and buys himself a cushy rider, though the extent of his labor is circling around and around on a lawn that, oddly enough, was just mowed the day before. While your back is breaking as you are washing windows, hanging off a ladder, he's humming along to his iTunes—deliberately not making eye contact so as not to see the steam coming out of your ears—and certainly can't hear you over the motor of his lawn toy. That's my personal experience, so I know this can and will happen, if you let it. And don't fall for the line, "Honey, I let you scrub the tub and toilet because you are so good at it."

It is not a gender preference when it comes to who likes the house or apartment to be neater. This can be either one of you. If one has a strong feeling about a well-organized home, and the partner either doesn't feel strongly either way, then most likely the home can maintain a neat and orderly décor. If your partner now agrees with a neat and orderly home environment but didn't exactly live in one, be careful opening the coat closet after they have offered to help: AVALANCHE!

The way one cleans versus the other's idea of tidy and neat may be drastically different. Conversations about how you each prefer the environment maintained, or how you each benefit from being more aware of those preferences, will save a lot of frustration later. So before you both go into action, define neat and orderly, and it will save a clunk on the head from last year's ice skates.

Now that you have both agreed to share a home together, the reality is that neither one of you has another home to go to other than this one. Personal space, time alone, togetherness, day in and day out, day in and day out, day in and day out, day in…how do you feel? Sure, at first it's a major step. It is the natural, progressive step, and family and friends are excited for you too. Your first dinner party gets planned; everyone comes over, bearing housewarming gifts, bottles of wine, oohing and aahing about how nice the place looks and how cute you both are. You're both glowing, and both of you have now been promoted to adulthood. Newsflash: this does not necessarily turn you into an adult. Making it work, places you in adulthood. And only time can be the true measure of this.

Now that you have both agreed to share a home together, the reality is that neither one of you has another home to go to other than this one. Personal space, time alone, togetherness, day in and day out, day in and day out, day in and day out, day in … Making this work places you in adulthood.

What are the general pros and cons of living together; the good and the not so good:

GENERAL PROS AND CONS OF LIVING TOGETHER	
PROS	**CONS**
Shared time together	Too much time together
Experimenting on getting to know each other	Discovering bad habits
Next step in the relationship	Too soon to live together
Sex more regularly available	Potential of lack of desire
Shared expenses	Difficult to exit out of the relationship
Use the space below to add to the list	

♂ – DON

18 – Cohabitation

Are you trying the cow before buying the milk?

I think there is no better way to learn more about your partner than by living with her. This is a great way to get more serious without heading straight into marriage. Getting into marriage and making that commitment without living with her is similar to buying a guitar without ever playing it, and before you play it, saying you are committed to playing it every single day for the rest of your life. WHAT! Does that even make sense? How do you know you will like playing it every day for the rest of your life? What if you play it and you hate it? When you look at it from that perspective, I really wonder how people could get married and live together until death without ever testing it out. The only difference may be arranged marriages because there are no emotions when making the selection. The parents do the selecting, and they do it based on what they know about their children.

Some people may be of the belief that those things can be worked out, but I say if you are going to make that commitment with someone, don't you want to have the best chance possible of succeeding? The reason for writing this book is to try to give people the insight about what is in store for them with a long-term relationship and marriage. I want every couple to succeed, have the absolute-best chance of succeeding, and have the tools at their disposal to make a commitment they made to each other a reality. Don't you want that chance? If you said yes, and why would you say otherwise, then COHABITATE!

Here are some of the major things you will learn when you cohabitate:

- You will get a better sense as to the frequency of sex, and if things start to slow down, think about how much they will slow down after marriage and then after kids. Are you prepared for a sexless marriage?
- You may decide to start sharing money. Does she want to pay less for the apartment because you are making more? Does she believe in sharing everything evenly? These clues and others may become apparent when you cohabitate.
- You also will get a glimpse of whether or not she will nag you, bother you, and want to change you. Don't think she doesn't want to change you. Women care more about the little things, and she will try to change things about you. She may be able to hold out until you're married, but just be wary of this because you can gain some valuable insight before you take the plunge.
- What is the expectation about the household chores? Well, this is a good place to test that out. Do you split the chores evenly or do you both work together, cook together, clean together, and do the laundry together? If you are the type whose mommy did everything for you and you expect this to continue with your girlfriend, you'd better be ready for an uphill battle. She will most likely accommodate you in the beginning, but this will wear thin after some time.

The minor things can be just as important because they will become little annoyances that will grow and grow and grow. Here are some of those things:

- Now that you live together, she never wants to go out.
- She may be a neat freak.
- On what side of the bed does she like to sleep?
- Is she a messy person?
- Does she follow you around cleaning after you?
- Does she redo things around the house that you already did?
- Does she invite friends over without consulting you?
- Do you find her on the couch every night playing on her phone?
- Or maybe she sees you every night playing Wii.

As you can see, cohabitation can tell you a lot about the woman you have chosen. These things may seem like nothing to you now, but wait until you are living this on a daily basis. You will understand how you can get completely annoyed, and you will find that when things are not going well in the relationship, the minor things really start to matter.

19 – Modern Marriage

Who wears the pants?

Roles have changed over the last century. Today, more than 40% of women are working and have college degrees. Many men are losing their positions, and because women might replace them, this could result in more men staying home, raising the children. Women are almost at an equal pay rate, and soon should be, especially if they are going to be the main breadwinner in the home and if expenses keep increasing.

With women giving birth and going back to work soon after, it has been very difficult for some of them who thought that they, instead of their partners, would be home raising their children. And men who are raising the children are not exactly prepared to be the at-home parent. This has been a new transition for both partners. As the trend continues to climb, both partners will need to embrace it in order for the relationship to work and remain successful. This is possible.

When one partner finds that satisfying job or career, each can enjoy and gain satisfaction in it, reducing the disappointment that most couples feel when one is forced into the responsible role as head of household. Having satisfaction with that career will increase the good feelings you can both share with each other.

Staying home to take care of the household has led men to feel displaced and less confident. **The scenario of traditional roles is rapidly disappearing and modern roles are emerging.** Men are designed by nature to be industrious. When this is not available or accessible, men can lose their sense of value and self-worth, which can lower their libido, their self-esteem, and their ambition to redirect. As a couple, it's important for both of you to share your feelings when it comes to your roles and expectations.

Discussion about what you and your partner will do and how you both will feel is important because the scenario of traditional roles is rapidly disappearing and modern roles are emerging.

You may have grown up in a two-income family. Perhaps it was by choice that both of your parents worked; perhaps each of your parents had a greatly satisfying career that they did not want to give up; or perhaps neither of your parents was able to cover the expenses alone.

Whichever the case, the roles in your household were set. Due to your upbringing, you may have your own ideas about what you envision for your family one day, and it might be the opposite of your childhood experience. If you were raised in a two-income family, you might instead believe that one parent should be home with the children, not dropping off your infant with a babysitter or nanny. Or perhaps you are in agreement with the way you were raised in a two-income family, and you will most likely continue with the same. Have you asked your partner what they are imagining? What if their upbringing was the opposite? Mom never worked outside the home but cared for the children at home; Mom was there when they got home from school; they were not a latchkey kid, and that is not an option in the future of their family.

Modern marriage has seen many changes, including multiracial, same-sex, and non-traditional living arrangements. Rarely do we now see couples marrying right out of high school. Yet what we see are individuals graduating from college and moving back home, perhaps living under their parent's roof until they are ready to marry. There is also the current trend that couples move out from their parental homes to live together but then circumstantially have to move back to one of their parent's homes to save money. Life, family, and preparing for a secure future take money, planning, and sacrifice.

Modern marriage is still a financial contract, broken only by suing the other spouse. There is now "no-fault divorce," which means neither party can claim "grounds" for divorce and win a settlement, as they once could. Today's family court does not hold any one spouse responsible for the breakdown of the marriage, whereas a spouse could once sue for divorce.

With marriage counselors, sex therapists, and divorce mediators now intervening as a means to repair or reconstruct the relationship, both parties are viewed from the perspective of their strengths. Each party is now seen as independent, resourceful, and able to pull their own weight.

Women have come a very long way in the past century. It was a mere 100 years ago, give or take a decade, that if a marriage dissolved, the man would be awarded full custody of the children born to the marriage. Women had no rights and were placed in the same category as children, referred to as chattel. Women could not gain custody of their children because they were not offered opportunities to develop viable, marketable skills that would enable them to hold a job or be employable. Today, there are more women than men earning a higher degree after high school. Not bad for the sisterhood. This is why women need to select a mate much more carefully. The need to marry for financial security no longer exists. This concept bears no weight. The problem is that, when children come into the marriage, one of the parents tends to be the primary caretaker, and if both parents are working, at least one of the them needs to have more flexibility in their job in case the child is home sick; or for school meetings, after school activities, summer vacation from school, and so on. Women are more apt to choose to be the primary caretaker. It's natural, but holding higher degrees lands them more secure and responsible jobs, squeezing out the men.

> **The problem is that, when children come into the marriage, one of the parents tends to be the primary caretaker, and if both parents are working, at least one of the them needs to have more flexibility in their job to accommodate the children's needs.**

With this switch and with limited job opportunities, men are left out in the cold, or rather, stagnant at home with the children, looking for work and trying to gain momentum while scurrying around caring for young children, tending to their many needs. Switching gears to professional goals while cleaning spaghetti off the walls and toilet training makes for a very stressful day. Men are loving, nurturing fathers, but assuming the role of primary caretaker has never been their instinct, not to mention that men are not by nature wired to multi-task. A man's brain is wired to compartmentalize. This has given them the ability to be leaders, separating their personal lives from their professional lives. Whereas women encounter and handle personal and professional obligations intertwined all day. Most women, while working, think and talk about their home lives. Men? Not so much. If men encounter an emotional situation about a conflict or a problem, they are more apt to problem solve, get through it, and move on. This may explain how much easier it is for a man to initiate make-up sex soon after an argument

So if your marriage results in dad being home with the children because of unemployment, loss of job, lack of opportunities, or because the gender pendulum has swung to the other side, you and he have the ability to adapt to social changes, as you need to, in order to maintain success in your relationship and reach a higher degree of expanded living and perspective.

From the beginning of time starting with the cave man, most women have been conditioned to expect the man to provide. His job was to battle, kill, and skin the wild boar and mammoths of his day, bringing meat and warmth to his cave woman. Men have been conditioned to expect the woman to then take the meat and skins and do something useful with them. It's difficult to say how long it took both caveman and his cavewoman to figure out they could eat the meat and wear the skin. Who knows if their first team effort resulted in the reverse. Maybe they tried to eat the skin and wear the meat. The good news is they figured it out and here we

In today's modern marriage, it no longer matters who battles the wild boar and who wears the skins; what matters is that the team can still get the job done and evolve.

are. In today's modern marriage, it no longer matters who battles the wild boar and who wears the skins; what matters is that the team can still get the job done and evolve.

Women have complained that their men are not providing for the family as they once did, and as a result, men have felt demeaned and robbed of confidence, and the women no longer desire them as they once did. This is a dilemma. The inability to adapt to new changes in society will only keep us stagnant and prevent us from evolving as a human race, and it is that evolution of human existence, according to many historians, anthropologists, scientists, and psychologists, which has been quite extraordinary up to now. Recent studies have shown that the male testosterone level has been decreasing. Fighting the saber-tooth tiger is no longer a need; therefore, the levels of this hormone are diminishing. This doesn't mean that you and your partner will be fighting over the same dress. That won't be the case, but perhaps it will be for your great-grandchildren. It will be normal by then, so don't gasp. Until then, if you and your partner are going to keep the human race from extinction, it's necessary to be open-minded as the world we live in continually changes. Expansion leads us toward survival.

What is equality when it comes to a relationship? Thinking about your relationship or about past relationships may have brought you to reflect on the equality and balance that are needed. It may never be 50/50 all of the time. The key is for it to fluctuate. Equality in a partnership has much to do with the distribution of love, attention, respect, time, devotion, and whatever it takes for both of you to feel secure. A relationship requires each of you to give 100% of your love, respect, communication, and understanding. When you give 100% and your partner gives 100%, what happens? Each of you is receiving 100%. Realistically, the goal is for you both to get your needs met. Is it fair to say they will always be met? No, but when you do know what it takes to make your partner happy, then giving should be natural.

Equality is the balance of female and male energy. Each of us has a portion of both. Depending on the circumstances in your relationship, you may feel or act more feminine, and then given another circumstance, your male energy may emerge. The same applies to him. What we would consider as demonstrating feminine energy is when your man cries and expresses vulnerability. How do you feel when this happens? Can your comforting be accepted? Does he show these emotions or hide them, or worse, bottle them up? How about you? Are you able to feel an array of emotions, including masculine ones? Do you recognize them, and can you and your partner be comfortable with such expressions as navigating your own goals; being industrious; being able to earn your own income by your decisions? Killing a bug?

Equality allows for growth in both directions. There are no limits to what each of you can do for yourself, for each other, and for the relationship. There are no rules based on gender. It is a custom-designed relationship, sculpted by both.

If you ever hear him say to someone else, "It's not up to me; she's the boss," and he may be saying it in jest, poke him with a stick anyway.

Even joking can send the message that there is a hierarchy

> **Equality allows for growth in both directions. There are no limits to what each of you can do for yourself, for each other, and for the relationship. There are no rules based on gender. It is a custom-designed relationship, sculpted by both.**

here. And you do not want that; don't even kid around. Roles are safe. Many relationships work well when roles are clear. These do not take away from the equality. Roles based on strengths and interests rather than gender will help maintain and avoid social stigma. When or if children are in the future or are here already, equality in the relationship will certainly send positive role-modeling messages. And as boys and girls grow up learning they are free to develop any and all skills and follow any interest they choose, it will raise their self-esteem and give them the confidence for success in what they feel is the right fit for them. As the pendulum swings toward the modern marriage, equality is going to meet its challenge.

♂ – DON

20 – Modern Marriages

Do you feel like you are giving up your man card?

Today's marriage is definitely different from marriages of the past. Roles in the family have become blurred. In the past, a husband knew exactly what to do and what was expected of him, and gender roles were clear and extremely comfortable for both sides. As a man, you would have been the breadwinner of the family, and your wife would have been home taking care of the kids. She also would cook, do laundry, and clean the house. As the man, you would be taking care of everything outside of the house: mowing lawns, taking out the garbage, and making home repairs. In terms of raising the children, the fathers were the disciplinarians.

Times have definitely changed, and in most cases, those changes have put a strain on marriages. The marital roles have shifted, and women and men are now burdened with the challenge of trying to make this shift in society. Many more women are working, and because of the recession that began in 2008, some women have become the bread-winners of the family. Many men lost their jobs and were forced into becoming domestic dads. For years, women have been fighting for equality, but now they have been thrust into this new role of bringing home the bacon. As a man, I would suspect that this does not feel good. Men want to be the saviors, the knights, the industrious ones who take care of everyone financially. Now, the big man on campus stays at home and takes care of the kids while the woman he married is working and is the only one earning an income.

In most cases, this not only does not feel good, but worse, your wife may be jealous that you are home with the kids, and YOU are feeling like a complete loser. This puts an extreme burden on the marriage. You don't feel good about not having a job and making more money, and your spouse may not feel good about that as well. She may feel you are not trying hard enough to get a job. However, you know that it feels like everything has dried up and you are sending out resumes that are going into a black hole. Yes, you feel like a loser, and your wife may be telling you that you ARE a loser. Your emotional connection has ended, there is no sex, and the marriage is at the brink of destruction. You may feel like this could never happen to you, that you are on top of the world. But as a mediator, I have seen a lot of marriages fail because of this scenario of the wife calling the husband lazy. Let's say that you are living together now and are not married or you are thinking about marriage. You need to discuss this scenario and determine how things would play out. You have to be honest and not just say what you think is right, but what you really feel. Your honesty with your partner and her honesty with you could save both of you a lot of heartache in the future.

In any case, the man's role as the breadwinner in the family is definitely diminishing. More women are graduating from college, getting higher degrees than men, and are earning more money. I think there may still be more work to do in terms of gender equality, but we have come a long way. Does your partner make more than you now? Would you be OK if she made more? Would you be OK being a stay-at-home dad while your wife earns the money? Some may say a resounding YES, but make sure you know yourself. It looks good on the outside, but it may not feel so good if you were actually doing it.

Whatever your situation, whether living together or getting married, the reality for you is most likely one of a two-earner household. Both of you will work, and you will be expected to do your fair share around the home. That means laundry, cooking, and other things that may have felt like the woman's responsibility in the past. Step up to the plate, and do whatever you can to equally share in all the domestic duties because it is only fair for both of you, even though you may have grown up with a mother who did all the domestic chores around the house. There is no expectation of anyone having a certain role in today's society. The future of gender roles can go in any direction; meanwhile, I know from traditional thinking that we may be sharing the roles, but we may not feel right while doing them. As a man, you need to accept this new society, embrace it, and make it work for you. It can be a very rewarding experience to share in those things with your partner.

> **In the reality of today's two-earner households, both of you will work, and you will be expected to do your fair share around the home. As a man, you need to accept this new society, embrace it, and make it work for you. It can be a very rewarding experience to share in those things with your partner.**

In order to understand your challenges with your partner, you need to understand what type of household she grew up in. Was her father the breadwinner of the family? Was her mother the caretaker who never worked? Did she come from a household in which both the mother and the father worked? Did her mother have a part-time job only while the kids were in school? Did her father help out around the house with the cooking, cleaning, and taking care of the kids? So when you ask her about how she feels about different situations during your marriage, don't accept her words spoken from cerebral reflection because her future actions and thoughts will be derived instinctively from how she was raised. The same goes for you. Even though you may think it is fair to do an equal amount of work around the home, your upbringing will determine how you actually feel about it, and you may resent doing this in the future. Make a pact with your partner that even though you know you have your biased view and she has her biased view, whatever they are, you will work through these issues to make it fair for both of you. This way resentment does not grow over time in the marriage, causing it to disintegrate.

♀ – DANA

21 – Parenting

Is he a dad or a father?

A few years back, I wrote my first book on parenting, *Please Don't Buy Me Ice Cream, a Child's Rules for Priceless Parenting*. The style of the book relates to the parent from a young child's point of view. This is the age when children look up to their parents and have a dependency on them. My second parenting book will be from the voice of adolescents and its title is *Please Don't Talk to Me, a Teenager's Rules, Period*. The first book was a joy to write, as younger children are still impressed by their parents and believe much of what we tell them. Teenagers will challenge everything we say and are not impressed by us as much. Or at least they won't admit it. My daughters are teenagers now. Recently, I was asked by my youngest to use an alias if I ever planned on visiting her school. And to think I have given them the best years of my life!

Parenting is like no other experience. You can tell, because when you are at a BBQ or a house party and the conversation hits on kids, everyone in the circle who has kids will suddenly perk up with, "Oh, you don't know what I go through; let me tell you what my kid did!" You will hear one of two stories: either the kid is a child genius who apparently will be a Rhodes Scholar, according to the parent; or the story will determine that the child will send his parent to a mental institution tomorrow with a nervous breakdown. Parents love to brag about their kids, and it becomes sickening. But we, as parents, must take pride in our kids. For most of us, the way the children turn out is a direct reflection on us. Or so we think or fear.

If you have children or are considering having children and you believe that their success or demise is a result of parenting, then you may want to take a look at the following basic parenting styles, which can make or break you as a parent.

If you have children or are considering having children and you believe that their success or demise is a result of parenting, then you may want to take a look at the following basic parenting styles, which can make or break you as a parent.

Generally there are three major parenting styles. The first is authoritative, the second is called affirmative, and the third is known as laissez-faire.

AUTHORITATIVE parenting is the discipline in which the parent, caretaker, or guardian rules with one-sided domination, with no room for opinion from the child. It's the authority's way or the highway. No one else gets to state their wants. An authoritarian's discipline once included corporal punishment, as in the bible axiom "Spare the rod, spoil the child," which was not going to happen in my household. Corporal punishment once looked like getting whipped with a belt, kneeling on rice, standing while holding a heavy stack of books, sitting in a corner, going to bed without dinner, being smacked, spanked, punched, tied up, and that sort of thing. Since the 1960s, these punishments have been considered cruel, abusive, and criminal.

Children who endure such harsh treatment are now being protected by laws and agencies, such as Child Protective Services. Children who are found with bruises are suspected as being victims of child abuse. CPS now investigates the caretakers and can, by law, remove the child from the home, place them in foster care, and arrest the perpetrator. Anyone in a certain group of specified professionals, like a police officer, social worker, or school administrator, is mandated to an ethical and professional responsibility of reporting suspicion and/or evidence. Children and parents must abide by this law, and if lines have been crossed and bruises, burns, or marks are discovered to have been due to discipline, a criminal police report is imminent.

Parenting books, lectures, workshops, and networking have become staples in modern society. Most everyone understands the detrimental effects of child abuse. Psychological child abuse is as harmful. And even though psychological abuse does not leave physical marks, this abuse leaves long-lasting scars on a child's self-esteem or self-worth and spawns poor school performance, substance abuse, criminal behavior, anti-social behavior, and the like. Both types of abuse must be treated in order to prevent serious dysfunction and a generational cycle. Authoritative discipline is the mind-set of a parent who may have their own scars and traumas from childhood. The need to control, intimidate, hurt, and degrade comes from a dark place of rage, fear, and poor self-control. With all the information that is now available and the laws that have been implemented to protect children, parents who continue to use this form of parenting today may be reported to child protective services. There are parents who feel that today's children are more spoiled and have more power because of the ban on corporal punishment. Those parents have lost their clarity and competency as disciplinarians. One parent in the household may have grown up in an authoritative home and may either rule in the opposite way or maintain that harsh discipline was the most effective. There are parents who were disciplined by the belt and have vowed to raise their child without physical punishment, never hitting, yelling, or using verbal criticism. These parents choose one of the next two styles.

AFFIRMATIVE parenting eliminates harsh, corporal discipline and the authoritative manner. This generally looks like, sounds like, and almost is balanced with equality, while having the parent still as the leader and authority. The difference is that the parent does not believe that their word must always be the final word but allows the child to express his or her feelings toward the matter. For example, the child wants to stay up a little later because of something they enjoy doing. The child can express himself or herself and explain what it is they want from the parent. The parent then feels that the child may or may not have a reasonable request, and they will either negotiate, if it's fair, or the parent will enforce the rule. The big difference is that the parent and the child both feel that their feelings and positions toward the matter are honored and respected, unlike the authoritative parent who considers the child's feelings or position as insignificant. The benefit to the child is that they're learning to follow rules, and that's that. Affirmative parents believe that children learn best when taught to explore their own feelings and ultimately develop the ability to make choices for themselves while feeling respected, not humiliated. Abused children lack self-esteem, having not been respected or encouraged to express themselves as well as having lived in an oppressive and fearful environment. Affirmative parenting recognizes the need for a child's self-esteem and a safe environment to express himself or herself.

LAISSEZ-FAIRE – The next parenting style is referred to as **laissez-faire**. Laissez sounds like lazy and it's not fair, although parents who practice this are typically non-parenting parents. They take very little initiative or responsibility in raising their child. The child may see this as quite fair since they are given so much freedom, yet this freedom is clearly neglect. Children who grow up having to raise themselves are lacking the necessary role modeling that parents provide. This can come in the form of structure, health, and guidance, such as nutritional, medical, mental, and educational. Children are not taught self-discipline mostly because parents lack self-discipline. A laissez-faire parental style in the home may result in the child's inconsistent school attendance or maintenance of jobs, and a lack of ethics, reliability, or respect for others and themselves. We see this parenting style when the parent navigates their way toward being the friend to their child more than the parent figure or role model. Children have friends and don't need their parent as a peer, they need their parent.

When exploring parenting styles with your partner, it's telling how each of you may embrace one of these three mentioned styles. One style does not fit all. In other words, either or both of you may feel strongly toward one or a combination of two. Exploring the description of each style at least allows for the communication to begin. You or your partner may not know how they will parent until children come into the picture. Do not, I repeat, do not be convinced that your partner will be a great parent because you see him with other kids. Having a great rapport with kids other than his own does not place him in the great dad arena. When they are someone else's kids, it is a lot different than when they are your own. When children are yours, it's up to you to get their needs met, raise them, nurture them, educate them, structure them, guide them, cry with them, dry their tears, cause their tears, argue with them, laugh with them, buy for them, buy for them, buy for them, and spend on them—all this while lacking sleep, sacrificing your own once-enjoyed pastimes, and trading them for trips to the playground, birthday parties, early nights to bed, compromising partnership priorities, and learning to accept advice, to forgive yourself for mistakes and, for the 21 years you care for them, expecting nothing in return—because it was your choice to bring them into the world, whether you planned them or not.

Many couples do not really know how challenging parenthood is. Suddenly you are catapulted into real adulthood. This little person cannot manage on their own for a long time, and it's not only survival. It's the socialization, the environment, their health and well-being. Children with learning disabilities or special needs will require additional time, money, and resources. Children who are chronically ill with allergies, asthma, or weak immune systems may miss many days of school. The reality of rearing children is wrought with wonder and excitement along with angst, disappointment, and God knows what else.

A very wise 40-year-old man once told me, "I am too selfish to have children. I want my freedom to ski, travel, and spend my money on me." Well, that sounded pretty self-absorbed to me at first, but knowing how he has lived, he made a very responsible decision for himself. He met a beautiful, loving woman; married her; and together they live a happy, carefree life with two dogs in the mountains of Lake Tahoe. That man is my brother Frank, and he loves his nieces and nephews but didn't need any of his own.

Although, I would appreciate it if Uncle Frank could take my kids for a week or two, or three.

Children are a blessing, but they are not for everyone. Often parents and family of the couple place pressure to contribute a new addition to the family. If your mom wants to be a grandma and you're not ready to have kids, tell her to badger your sister. Do not let this pressure influence you. The excitement of a new baby in the family is only short-lived. The novelty is over before you want it to be. Remember, once you have them, you can't give them back.

Do not let family pressure influence you to have children. The excitement of a new baby in the family is only short-lived.

Bleak, discouraging words, you're right. But it's not all bleak or mentally draining; there are precious, prideful moments in each stage of their development as well as yours. Children will teach you things about yourself that you never knew and, at times, will trigger your own childhood memories, good and bad. Brace yourself. Before becoming a parent, it is a good idea to get right with your own childhood, so traumas are not passed on, or repressed and then acted on. For example, a parent's survival from a childhood wound can play out as they parent their own child. Often, parents are not aware of the dynamics of their family of origin until they are repeated in their own family. Yet, this time, the survivor of childhood is now the parent, and a whole lot of emotions and suppression can get kicked up. We hear parents who give in to their kids or indulge them with material things because they want their children to have the kind of childhood they themselves didn't have. Well, your kids don't know the absence of things or the neglect, but what they do know is lots of indulgence. Spoiling a child in order to make up for a parent's lost childhood often backfires, and the spoiled child will never appreciate much. They develop a bottomless appetite, and therefore nothing is ever satisfying or enough. The haunting desire to have more and more, that next thing, is an internal conflict you want to spare them.

Parenting is a responsibility. Unless you are really ready to commit and share this job with your partner wholeheartedly, as well as to make the sacrifices, then wait until you're sure and can agree on the type of parenting that you feel is best and that coincides with your present lifestyle. It's the children who suffer when it doesn't work.

$\male$ – DON

22 – Parenting

Is she a mom or a mother?

This is such a major topic in a marriage. When you bring someone into this world together, there could be no better way of growing your love and commitment to each other. Having children is the best thing that ever happened to me. I loved helping them grow and loved seeing them in each stage of their life. I continue to enjoy that part of my life and theirs. However, just because it worked for me does not mean it will work for you. Some couples might choose not to become parents, for a variety of reasons.

Think about the time when you were at your darkest moment or were completely exhausted. Can you visualize this? Does this happen on a regular basis or does this happen very rarely? Just so you know, when you feel this way, this is when the baby will be crying and you will have to get up and either change a diaper or feed and comfort the little one in some way. The baby will not care that you are completely exhausted from a long day at work. The baby will cry and cry and cry until he or she gets what they want and need. Are you prepared for that? Don't expect your wife to do this for you all the time, or maybe any time at all. Maybe the two of you decided it was best that you stay home to watch the children. It is always best to share in the responsibilities, especially if both of you are planning for her to go back to work after the baby is a few months old.

Be wary of the wife who wants to stay home with the child. From my experience, this can only hurt you and the children later. A wife who stays home can be trouble. Now here is where I will try to be brutally honest without causing a complete uproar to all the stay-at-home moms.

When I say trouble, I mean that some women just do not want to work. They will keep having babies so that they do not have to go to work. I have heard some call this the "anchor baby." Don't get me wrong; staying at home with the children can be a great experience for the mom. It could also help the dad focus on work because he knows that things are being handled at home. There are some moms who are fantastic with the children; they are constantly helping to enrich them in various different ways. And let's face it, who cares more about those children than a parent (in most cases)?

> **Be wary of the wife who wants to stay home with the child. This can only hurt you and the children later. Some women just do not want to work. They will keep having babies so that they do not have to go to work. I have heard some call this the "anchor baby."**

When I say trouble, I also mean that the rumor mills are usually started by a stay-at-home parent. The gossip just churns and churns and has no positive effect on anyone, but someone is always getting hurt. It is a useless and unproductive way to spend life. In addition, if the children are old enough and mature enough to stay at home alone for a couple of hours, why not have the mom contributing financially to the household to ease the stress on dad, showing her children that women can be contributors in the work force.

Not only that, mom's mind may be energized, and she may have the opportunity to engage in more stimulating conversation.

However, the woman who wants to stay at home, even when the child is 17 years old and ready for college, may state that her child needs her help and could not function without her. The child may actually have after-school activities and not even come home until 5:30 p.m. They may say, "Do you want your child to fail or get into trouble?" just to guilt you into not pushing them to go back into the workforce. She gets used to not working and may continue to find excuses as to why she should not go back to work. You may get lucky and get the woman who wants and likes to go to work. She either is not obsessed with being a stay-at-home parent or would like to stay at home but realizes that that may be a luxury. And let's face it, wouldn't it be better if the child was socializing with other children their age and learning how to become independent? Seeing their mom as a high-powered executive isn't so bad either. In addition, mom will have something else to offer the children when she comes home: information from the outside! She has another world now that she brings to the children to help enrich them even more. How great is that!

As the child gets older, you will both start to realize the parenting style of each spouse. It is best to know the parenting style of your spouse because their parenting may frustrate you to death.

PARENTING STYLES

Generally, there are four types of parenting that people tend to exhibit with their kids. Depending on your family of origin, you may take on the style of your own parents or swing the other way. Many times people swing away from the way they were raised. Who is to say when the pendulum will swing back, if it ever does. In the meantime, the following are four styles that may be familiar to you, based on your parents. Understand your parent's style and then understand the parenting style of your partner's parents. Make a decision how you wish to parent. Some parents feel they are a little of each of these types, which is typical, but you should think about it, and the two of you should have the same style going into the marriage. If you disagree about your parenting styles before kids, it is highly likely you will have many fights during the marriage about the children and their future. Read ahead. Which style do you want to be?

Affirmative parenting is more a democratic style; parents are willing to listen to their children and be more responsive. Parents offer more support than punishment. These children grow up to self-regulate their thoughts and feelings because they are given the opportunity to think for themselves and be asked more about how they feel, even though they may not always get their way. They are encouraged to formulate their own opinions and ideas; however, they learn that their parents have the final say. These parents want respect and love.

Authoritarian parenting is characterized by strict rules, and for the child, any failure to abide by these rules results in punishment. Authoritarian parents don't feel the need to explain themselves when enforcing rules. This upbringing becomes a problem when the children become adults and find it very difficult to trust their own judgment, make decisions for themselves, or think independently. These children are disallowed to show emotion. Parents who rule under this style are usually the ones who believe they would rather be feared—they call it respected—than loved.

Laissez-faire parenting is not to be confused with the political economy term. The expression loosely applies to the sound of it: "lazy." The laissez-faire parent is uninvolved with or unaware of the responsibilities and importance of appropriate child rearing. These are the parents who fail to maintain structure and give the child the maximum amount of freedom, unaware that this is actually at the expense of the child's proper development. These children grow up to be spoiled, rebellious, irresponsible, and afflicted with psychological distress.

Indulgent parenting will have few behavioral expectations for the child. The parents are very involved with their children but set few demands, boundaries, or rules. These parents are nurturing, but very responsive to the child's needs and wishes, doing them a disservice. They do not let them think or do things on their own, thereby creating very dependent children. Indulgent parents do not require children to behave, which usually results in creating spoiled brats. These children tend to be more impulsive and expect to get their own way.

> Understanding the way you parent and choosing the outcome for your children is better parenting and better planning for your children's future. Knowing in advance how to make the necessary adjustments could mean a much better future for them.

Understanding the way you parent and choosing the outcome for your children is better parenting and better planning for your children's future. Knowing in advance how to make the necessary adjustments could mean a much better future for them—a future that finds them happy, instead of never finding happiness or looking for it in the wrong places.

THE LAW

It's also important to know the law about maintenance (alimony) in your area. If you have a spouse who does not want to work, what makes you think she will want to work if you get divorced? Check the law, because if you get divorced from this type of woman, watch out; she will take you for everything you have because she does not want to work. There are laws that require lifetime maintenance. OUCH! How would that feel after your wife cheated on you, then wants a divorce, and then gets lifetime maintenance to help support her and her new lover?

23 – Growth

*I'll take "Growth" for $500, please:
What is self-awareness?*

Insight, foresight, hindsight, and the awareness to develop as a person, separate from your partner, have benefits far beyond imaginable. Don't ever think that you have all the answers and have learned everything you need to know about yourself and your life. Those who choose to make life worth living and enriching are those who see that there is room to grow.

If your partner is not one to look within and believes that self-actualization is not necessary, you may need to keep looking for a new partner, unless you feel the same way. Many such people tend to be superficial and shallow, meaning they prefer to avoid a deep sense of existence. Conversely, there are those individuals who live by spiritual awakening, introspective analysis, psychology, philosophy, and soul searching as their main vein of being. Know where you are on the spectrum.

Existential	Metaphysical

▲

Know who your partner is and from where they acquire inspiration. If you are esoteric, but they believe that death leads only to darkness, chances are that the polarity will become a barrier to shared growth and development.

If soul searching and inspiration from the spiritual realm are not collective experiences, perhaps your growth is in the earthbound existence, and your goals are not about karma and eternal life but about what can be accomplished in the here and now. With that as a philosophy, both you and your partner can share goals and objectives that lead to material wealth, education and higher degrees, climbing of the career ladder, creativity, celebritism, and the entire fulfillment within your own talents and ambitions. Together you want to conquer the world; you want to make a difference; you know you are here for some purpose, not because God set your agenda, but because you know that just hanging around is insufficient and unsatisfying.

If you have this conversation with your partner about what you hope to achieve in your lifetime and get a negative response, take another look at your life with this person.

If you and your partner feel the same drive, that's wonderful, whether it's rescuing stray cats and dogs, volunteering for the auxiliary fire department, or running a corporation; making a film, becoming the next great actor, neurosurgeon, or the best writer; or at least publishing a novel that has been rolling around in your head for years. Having the right partner and having this conversation about what you hope to achieve in your lifetime indicates that the goals you have set for yourself can be realized. If you have this conversation with your partner, but you get a negative response like –"You're fantasizing or ridiculous for thinking you're so gifted or that you will follow through with resources to actually make any of your dreams come true"– then take another look at your life with this person. If you stay and do not accomplish the dream, you only have yourself to blame.

♂ – DON

24 – Growth

Which way will she grow?

When getting into a relationship with someone, you definitely want to know their ability to grow and also your ability to grow. There are people who wish to merely exist and get through life. They are happy with who they are, and they want to just continue to work the job they work and live life the way they live it. Then there are other people who are not happy unless they are constantly learning new things and growing and developing in various different ways. You'd better know these characteristics about yourself and your partner because it could very easily destroy that happy bond for you in the future, especially when you turn around years later and find that you have absolutely nothing in common.

There are multiple ways to grow. You could grow mentally, physically (which most of us do in the wrong way), spiritually, and emotionally. It is also possible for you to develop in one area and not another. For example, you may be interested in learning new things and love having intellectual conversations, but you do not care about developing physically, exercising, and staying active. That means you will never take care of your body and will only be feeding your mind. There are others that want to have complete balance in their lives, so they will want to grow in all four areas. As I said before, it is important that you know the area in which you will most likely grow and the same for your partner. It will make things much easier later in life.

It is important that you know the area in which you will most likely grow and the same for your partner. If you don't share each other's need to grow in any one area, then one of you may have an affair in that area.

In these four areas, I will tell you about the affairs you will have in each area, which become necessary to fill a void that your partner is not fulfilling. If you are the one who doesn't share your partner's need to grow in any one area, then your partner may have an affair in that area. That's right, I said it. If you are not filling this need for your partner, they will stray and have an affair in any one or more of these areas. That does not mean a physical affair, but it means the affair with someone else or something else to fill this need they have.

MENTAL GROWTH

Do you or your partner love to talk about intelligent subjects? Maybe you like going to lectures or talking about politics. Is it important that you keep your mind active? If this is you and you marry someone who does not want to be intellectually stimulated, you will have trouble in the marriage. When you are alone together, if this ever happens, you will want to talk about new, interesting things, and your partner will be stuck in the same old mind-set. After a while you will look for other outlets to get what you are looking for. You will have a mental affair outside of the relationship. This affair may take the shape of many different forms. You may find that you or your partner are talking to other intellectuals or attending lectures without the other party. Also, you may find that you have friends who are more intellectual as well. The next thing you know is that you and your partner are miles apart and have very little to talk about. The one who is growing mentally will not be interested in the other partner anymore, and this in turn will put a strain on the relationship.

PHYSICAL GROWTH

This is a difficult one because some people may never want to develop the physical side of themselves until one day they have a heart attack or someone close has a heart attack or dies. All of a sudden they want to improve themselves physically. I say this is difficult because neither of you may be physically motivated or interested in improving physically, but there may be an intervention in the future that pushes you or your partner into wanting this for themselves. And then a divide may start to occur between you. If this divide starts to happen, are you then prepared to make the choice to start developing this area with your partner? If you don't, you run the risk of losing that partner to someone else who does believe that the physical side is important.

SPIRITUAL GROWTH

Do you know your partner's and your spiritual side? Are you religious? Is your partner religious? The difference between spiritual and religious is that a spiritual person believes in God, but follows no traditions or does not go to services on a regular basis. Some people are very religious, and they need to go to services and follow all the rituals of their religion. They do not feel comfortable with themselves unless they are following all those practices. Other people are happy they have God in their life, can talk to God any time they want, and do not have to follow any rituals or traditions. Then there are those who do not believe in spirituality at all. Know yourself and know your partner. Also know that at sometime in your lives, one of you may become religious or spiritual to help you get out of a crisis. This could definitely change the dynamic of your relationship. What would you do if you did not believe in God, but ten years into your relationship, your partner decides they want to be baptized and become "born again"? How would you handle this? What if the roles were reversed? Would you want your partner to convert with you or would you respect their beliefs? As I stated before, people will find like-minded people, and that's when the affairs start. They will gravitate to people who like the same things. So if one of you becomes very religious, it could add a lot of stress on the relationship. Take a look at your beliefs and those of your partner, and try to determine if this will be an issue for you in the future.

EMOTIONAL GROWTH

This area can be very important to people. If they do not feel emotionally connected, then everything else will suffer. They may feel you don't love them anymore, and you start growing apart. The disconnect starts with something simple and then becomes a mountain after days, weeks, and years of not resolving these issues. Usually when the parties do not have this connection, they will start to stray and find someone else who gives them the emotional connection they need: the need to connect, to communicate, to laugh, and to enjoy experiences together. Besides a sexual affair, some people may have an emotional affair and not be physical. They rationalize that the emotional part is

OK because it is not sexual or physical. This is definitely a lion in sheep's clothing because, if not resolved, it will continue to grow and will absolutely break up your relationship with your partner. You should both continue to grow emotionally and try to connect on deeper and deeper levels by understanding what makes each other happy, sad, angry, etc. Some people decide to never grow emotionally and stay together because the commitment is so strong. Know yourself and know your partner.

25 – Family

Will his past reveal the future?

When it comes to selecting the right partner, it's best never to underestimate your partner's family background. Asking questions in regard to his childhood is extremely essential for determining signs of childhood trauma; parental guidance; and values, such as education, career ambition, spiritual beliefs, or none at all. Have you had the opportunity to meet his extended family? Do you have a relationship with any member of his family? Many couples marry, never having met their partner's parent(s) until the wedding, or even later, when the baby is born.

You may want to investigate his background. Knowing the family history offers information about family themes, illnesses both medical and mental, financial wealth or ruin, secrets, suicide, abuse, or prison; or maybe he is related to a famous writer or scientist. Family heritage and cultural mores are sure signs of what is to come when children enter into the equation. Don't you know that 99% of those photos of children on the back of the

Never underestimate your partner's family background. Family heritage and cultural mores are sure signs of what is to come when children come.

milk carton are children who were abducted by divorced parents kidnapping and transporting them back to their home country? You may need to know if he has a history of mental illness in his genetic pool. If a relative committed suicide, there is a history of depression that may be passed on. Not to scare you, but what if the man you have fallen for is a transsexual? It has happened. It's not unusual for a woman with gender-identity conflicts to desire to have male body parts. You may not realize, nor has it been revealed to you, that your partner is a homosexual. He may know it but for whatever reason chooses to fight his natural urge; or he may be repressing it, and one event may trigger its emergence. Some women marry into this difficult relationship only to be told that he can no longer live with this lie and asks for a divorce. Find out and pay attention before it is too late. Oftentimes women have come to own their homosexual truths and leave the marriage after having children. Some men and women have hidden this, hoping that the urge of their sexual orientation will fade. But oftentimes, because of fear of judgment and coming out, they live their lives as silent sufferers. Help him or her come to the truth within themselves before it's too late and loved ones end up hurt or bitter.

During the years that a couple dates and lives together, not much of the real, important information gets transferred. It's OK to talk about personal feelings long before engagement. Roles are pretty well established by the time the wedding takes place, and most friends and family can predict the portrait of the new couple and their relationship personality. Little do they, or you, know the intricacies of who you are, together and apart.

This might very well come from each other's family personality. One mirrors, for various reasons, the characteristics of someone in the family. It's important for a couple to visit with extended family, not for just holiday cheer and gift exchange, but a real sit down. You really need to know what your boyfriend was like growing up. Demand to see photos; ask to know the history of the family. Who came from the old country and why? Who was married to whom; how and when did children come into the family? Is there a bias to one gender; is there favoritism; and is there a black sheep? Does one hold all the anger, the sadness, and the secrets? Who is the needy one of the family? You may wonder how you ask these questions and not sound like you're writing the family's biography. It's OK to be curious about the family; it doesn't mean you're overly suspicious, and it may be thought of as a compliment that you are naturally interested in all the family, their health, their traditions, their idea of a happy family event and their possible sadness or tragedy.

It's important for a couple to visit with extended family, not for just holiday cheer and gift exchange, but a real sit down. You really need to know what your boyfriend was like growing up.

You also want to know if there has been domestic violence; has anyone spent jail time, was there a homicide? A family at any economic or educational level can have a serial killer among their kin, so you might want to ask if your boyfriend's or girlfriend's relative, uncle, cousin, sibling, or aunt on up to grandma has acted out in such a way that society might frown upon. While looking at the photos that you volunteer to view one night while all of you are sharing a casual evening at his mom's, ask about the guy in the photo: "Who is he?" If the room gets silent, you are on to a family secret. Press on. Ask, "Where is he now?" If it takes them a few minutes to answer, keep a mental note. And that's how you find out. It's usually a relief when you find out that the one in the photo was the well-known neurosurgeon who operated on Neil Armstrong or some other famous contributor whom he saved. Or his aunt was the Chief Justice of the Supreme Court. Either way, outlaws or celebrities, it does not necessarily define your boyfriend, but the family stories are the legacies that have shaped and formed the family's definition of themselves.

Maybe your boyfriend is the rebel of the family, which means he was cut out of the inheritance. Or maybe he is the loyal son awarded all of grandmother's inheritance. Maybe his only sibling was the honor student who was given college tuition and your boyfriend wasn't, and he harbors resentment or shame among his parents and family. Perhaps his mother was the oldest of twelve, who was expected to raise her siblings and, by the time she was 17 years old, had had enough and ran off to marry the first boy she dated, got pregnant with your boyfriend, never taking time for herself, catering to him as if on automatic pilot, and now he is an adult who can barely boil water or wash a pot.

As I said at the beginning of this chapter, never underestimate the importance of knowing your partner's family background!

26 – Family

Will her past reveal the future?

When trying to understand your partner, there are a lot of clues that come from your partner's family values. These values were the ones that she grew up with, and they were essentially what developed that person into who they are today. Understanding the family values will help you understand the place that your partner came from and what shaped them and made them who they are today.

RESPECT: Did your partner grow up with a family who respected each other or was it everyone fending for themselves? When people grow up in a household where there is mutual respect and everybody is looking out for each other, then you most likely have a partner who will respect you. If you know your partner grew up in a family who treated each other badly, stealing boyfriends or girl-friends, or hurting each other's feelings and not caring, you will have a lot to deal with. This person will not know what it is like to respect you and the new family you are creating together. It may also be true that your partner wants something different, even though she grew up in such an environment, and does not choose this for herself. Be careful because words do not always match behavior. Watch for the signs.

RESPONSIBILITY: Did your partner have a family in which everyone had chores and pulled their own weight, or was it a situation in which everything was done by the parents who never asked for help from the kids? This partner will most likely expect you to do things for them and will not do their fair share around the house. Growing up and learning responsibility at a young age helps tremendously in life when working and when in a relationship. When you call, they return your phone call; they meet you when they say they are going to meet you, etc.

HONESTY: Know if the household your partner grew up in was a household of honesty or if everyone just lied to everyone else for their own benefit. Did they take accountability for their actions, stand up, and say they were sorry for what they did? The reverse is someone who is always blaming other people for what they did; they will blame you for things they did as well. It is difficult being with someone who will not be truthful with you. Trust is the foundation of every relationship. Without it you cannot be safe or feel safe.

PART OF A GROUP: It is a great feeling to be part of something bigger. A family that helps each other out is there for each other when the chips are down and picks up the pieces when you have fallen. It gives you a sense of power when fighting the world. It can be difficult for someone who feels alone and does not have a support team to assist them. It is much easier for a person to have confidence in themselves when they know they have a whole team backing them up.

TRADITIONS: You should know your partner's traditions and be prepared to honor those traditions as best you can. If you have conflicting traditions, then compromise and share in those of each other. Switch off every other year, or do what it takes to help them continue.

COMMUNICATION: How does your partner communicate with their family? Do they discuss feelings and emotions openly? Do they keep everything bottled up? Do they talk about anything real or just the weather?

PLAY TOGETHER: The family that plays together, stays together. Your partner may have grown up with a family that played board games every Sunday night. They took family vacations every year, and on Saturdays there were family activities, like going to the beach or the park. The reverse is if your partner grew up in a dysfunctional family and everyone did their own individual thing. They never did anything together. A person growing up in a household like this could be extremely hungry for a real family unit, or they could just want things to stay the same and never feel the need to do things together.

FLEXIBILITY: If your partner grew up as the only child in the family, they probably grew up faster because adults were always around. Most likely, they are also more selfish because everything was done for them and they got all the attention. Never doing without and never sacrificing could create a difficult challenge for them to have to share home life with someone else. Think about a family in which there are multiple children and everyone has a different schedule. You need to make adjustments and sacrifices, learning to be dynamic and going with the flow. You may have gotten your way once in a while, but you always had to adjust your thinking.

UNDERSTANDING AND TOLERANCE: Does your partner have family members who don't talk with each other or who hold a grudge? This will carry over to your life. They will think it is OK to just walk away when they have problems instead of facing the issues and dealing with them. You may have a partner who is very tolerant of things that happen and will understand things better when the chips are down. You want someone who helps you when you are at your worst, not who kicks you when you are flat on your face.

LOVE: How much love was in your partner's family? Was it OK to hug and kiss in public? Was it OK for the father to hug and kiss his sons? Are they always showing affection to each other? Watch how they interact when they are together, and see if there is a basis of love between her parents and the rest of the family.

DIVORCED FAMILY: This may tell you a few things about your partner. Did her parents divorce? If yes, what type of relationship did her parents have after the divorce? Did one parent get alienated from the other? This can be very telling and give you good insight into her feelings and thoughts.

As you can see, family values mean a lot and can tell you a bit about the future for you and your significant other. See the behavior, ask questions, and have an open mind. Discuss matters, and don't be in denial when you hear something that doesn't make sense. Build the communication. As the saying goes, "If you see something, say something." It could mean the difference between a great life, a ho-hum life, or a life of misery. What do you choose?

27 – Tragedy

Is he tough enough?

We all experience some degree of stress and adversity in our lives; this is a part of life with which we must contend. More significant is how we handle these times in our lives that challenge us and test our character. Think back on a time in your life that hurt you, made you very sad, or placed you in a dilemma that required the most enormous inner strength. How you handle yourself in these types of situations and understanding how your partner handles these situations could mean the difference between a supportive relationship or one that leaves you or your partner feeling alone.

Granted, one's typical day of losing their keys is not a disaster but maybe for your partner it is. Worse difficulties could be finances, loss of a job, being unemployed for a length of time, miscarriages, mental illness, sickness, extended family, and so on. When these sorts of stressful situations occur and you feel out of control or in deep sorrow, how do you manage? Whom do you go to first? What are the immediate emotions? Are they visible or do you bottle them up? Does your partner know how to support you during a difficult time? Have you experienced a difficult challenge together, and if so, how did both of you handle this?

Although no one wishes anyone bad days, it is important to have had a degree of adverse experience with your partner and to understand each other's capacity for empathy and resourcefulness. You really do not know exactly how you will support your partner or how he will support you. Paying attention and asking for what you need is essential for strengthening your relationship as time goes on. Do not assume that if you are having a horrible day—like your alarm didn't go off, your car then broke down, and your staff quit on you—that your partner knows how to console you. He doesn't unless you tell him how. There is nothing wrong with saying, "I had a really bad day, and it would be nice if you would sit there and listen to me gripe." You may want to be clear about whether you need him to listen and not advise. Men tend to want to problem solve, and sometimes you don't need an advisor. You just need him to stroke your hair and listen without hearing, "Well, did you check out the engine before you started the car?"

How you handle yourself in times of adversity and understanding how your partner handles these situations could mean the difference between a supportive relationship or one that leaves you or your partner feeling alone.

Ask your partner when he is having a bad day what he wants to hear or what he wants you to do. He may be the kind of man who keeps his problems and feelings to himself. Giving him the space to process and do his own problem solving as he is accustomed to doing is what he needs. You can offer a shoulder or encouraging words that could be welcomed and let him know you are available. We all process our pain in our own way.

By understanding your partner's needs and sharing your needs during a difficult time, either concerning a problem you share together or experience individually, the way you create a safe landing place is by listening deeply to your partner and honoring his experience. As you reach out to him in his time of need, allow him to reciprocate when the time calls for it.

A close friend married a man with brain cancer. He is 50 years old and she is 49. This was their second marriage, and both have children from previous marriages. The brain cancer is in remission and hopefully will remain so. The thought that the tumors could return and surgery is not an option has at times been the stressor that exacerbates what would seem a benign, healthy family matter into a sleepless night for this couple.

A couple who were living together, planning to marry, finds themselves suddenly dealing with an unexpected accident, leaving the girlfriend paralyzed.

Will your relationship survive a crisis? You can learn about your partner and yourself in regard to coping skills and resiliency in the wake of a disaster by taking note of the past experiences both of you have had.

These two examples are extreme and rare, but they happen. More often, the stressful situations that happen in a couple's lifetime are job loss, financial decline, illness, family loss, freak accidents, and the like. Will your relationship survive a crisis? You may not know until it happens. You can learn about your partner and yourself in regard to coping skills and resiliency in the wake of a disaster by taking note of the past experiences both of you have had. Have there been "bad-hair-day adversities" in your life? Have there been challenges that have forced you to expand your usual comfort level? Coping skills and resiliency are known to be developed by direct experience. However, resiliency has also been a birth trait. One never knows to what degree these coping skills and resiliency can strengthen and develop given the necessary processing.

As you and your partner share personal traumas that occurred throughout each of your lives, explore how each of you processed these difficult times. It's important to discover in your partner how they coped. Did they have family and friends to lean on, did they lean on anyone, or did they withdraw and go it alone? Are they still scarred by the misfortunes—have they grieved? Is there a repressed sadness—perhaps your partner or you yourself are mildly depressed? Have you assessed for depression? If anger and rage are at the surface and appear to be easily triggered but not rational, there could be depression lingering.

Explore the value and access to joy. Without joy in your life, there may be a feeling of hopelessness. If there is a feeling of hopelessness, there is a problem. Depression is generally described as a feeling that there is no future, that there is hopelessness and an inability to visualize a future, meaning one of joy and happiness, of peace and contentment. Has anyone in their family considered, attempted, or succeeded in suicide?

On a more positive note, check to assess your partner's or your ability to be optimistic. A woman once described her husband as so pessimistic that it didn't matter whether he saw the glass half full or half empty—he believed the glass would spill anyway. That's a negative Nellie. This you may want to know before you commit to a lifetime together.

A single man loved a woman he had been dating for a while and had thought to marry until he realized she was chronically depressed. He sought out therapy, psychiatrists, and activities whenever she sank into her depression. He would protect her, spend hours talking to her, but ultimately he felt he would not be able to manage a life with her, fearing that the depression would burden him to the extent that he would one day regret having a family and being the sole caretaker during her bouts of depression. He decided this when he realized that all his efforts of participating in couple's therapy, paying for her individual therapy, seeking psychiatrists, and traveling and initiating activities yielded no improvement, due to her resistance. He was aware that any improvement would have to now come from her desire to work through her depression, but it never really did. He also came to the realization that while he was focusing on her needs, he was neglecting his own. This led to loss of income, distraction from career, isolation from friends and family, and ultimately coming to the epiphany that he himself suffered with depression and ignored his, but lived vicariously through hers. Was he wise man? Yes. He projected into the future and saw massive dysfunction, knowing very well that there would have been children born to this marriage, and he just could not in good consciousness allow that to happen. The good news is that they are still very close friends.

When coping skills and the processing of tragedies lead to mental illness, the decision to stay or go must not be avoided. The biggest mistake couples make is that they believe these stressors will go away. They don't—they usually get worse. Is it important to ask your partner if there is mental illness?

Mental illness is genetic; it can be passed on throughout

generations. Know your bloodline and history and learn about your partner's.

Also, investigate how your partner and their family cope with tragedy. Has there been drinking, substance abuse, gambling, pornography, criminal behavior, homicide? Yes, homicide. One couple who were together fought often, and the woman would become violent. During episodes of fighting, she would attack him physically. He then learned that the woman he loved but whom he often fought with was a daughter of a murderer. This certainly gave him information on which to rest his head, without losing his head.

28 – Tragedy

Can she handle a bad-hair day?

Every one of us runs into tragedy or stress at least one time in our lives, but it is how we handle it that reveals our true character. Now ask yourself: have you had stress or tragedies occur in your life since you have been with your partner? This is an extremely important part of the relationship. How you handle yourself in these types of situations and understanding how your partner handles these situations could mean the difference between a great relationship and one that is hanging on by a thread. It also depends on how bad the tragedy is. If tragedy means you lost your keys or you just can't get your hair right that day, you have not run into tragedy.

What have been the stressors or tragedies in your life in the past? What have been those of your partner? When you run into a stressful situation, do you panic or are you calm? How about your partner? Do you appear calm on the outside but there is turmoil on the inside? Is your partner a hysterical mess whenever any little thing occurs in her life? Now that does not mean that she will be a hysterical mess if someone dies in the family. She may handle major tragedies with a calm, cool, collected view. Also, you should know if you are able to calm her down when she is getting hysterical or if you are the same basket case and you keep bringing each other down. Picture both of you with flailing arms and hands, running in all directions screaming at the top of your lungs.

The Basket Case

This is the one who handles every type of stressful situation, whether minor or major, with the calmness of a raging sea. She will scream at you, scream at everyone else, scream at herself. She may not even know how to calm herself down. She will pace up and down until she is utterly exhausted. The basket case is exactly that: a basket that has limited use and just sits there.

The Calm Storm

This is the type of person who will initially be OK. When tragedy strikes or if put into a stressful situation, they will handle everything with grace. After some time, this type will let it all out and be extremely vocal about what just happened. How would you handle this type of person? This may also be the person who has a storm inside of them, but on the outside they are as cool as a cucumber. When dealing with this one, you have to get them to talk and get those feelings out; otherwise, it will affect their health greatly because everything is bottled up inside. Are you the type of person who can do this for them? If you are this calm-storm type of person, will your partner help you get through this? Will she help you talk and communicate?

Even-Keeled

The even-keeled person will always act and feel the same. They take tragedy in stride like it was an everyday occurrence. They may say, "Shit happens." You will never get a rise out of this person. You could shout and shout at them, but they will never show you any anger. This could be extremely frustrating, but you should also know that if there ever was a major tragedy, this person would probably save your life. Not that it matters in your everyday life. If you are this even-keeled type and your partner is not, she may not understand this behavior. She may do everything in her power to get you angry. She may look at you like you don't even care, but you do care. You just have an extremely high tolerance for adversity. You could be a rescue worker because you would be calm and cool and your emotions would be in check while you logically work through the problems to keep everyone safe and sound. However, she will be extremely frustrated with you because she wants to see that you care, and anger or emotions seem to be the only way.

Tragedy can strike at any time in your life. Knowing how you and your partner will deal with this beforehand will help you both during that tragedy. It will help you cope, and it gives your partner the warning to know how to anticipate your behavior, actions, and words in any future circumstance.

29 – Infidelity

How to keep it cheat proof?

Will he cheat on you? He may. Will you cheat on him? You might. Don't underestimate the possibility. When you both committed to the relationship and labeled it exclusive, what exactly did that mean to each of you? Let's face it, many couples have taken that vow of being faithful to each other, but we all know how that turns out.

So how do you keep your relationship cheat-proof? It has something to do with who you are within yourself. Is fidelity a virtue you uphold on your own? If being faithful means that you would never betray the one you profess your love to, then that is your rule and your moral principle. This doesn't mean you are a pure and holy being; you may have other rules you justify breaking.

Rules are the standard but rules also bend. I am often amazed that when I'm on the subway platform waiting for the train, I think of how many thugs mug people and gangs shoot at each other on the platform yet don't break the NO SMOKING law. So bending the rules or following them according to our standards seems to make most sense. And when we need to bend the rules or even break them, we go into the back closet in our head, rummage through a pile of justifications, and select one.

As a species, our main modus operandi is to survive; we struggle to get our needs met. If we don't find peace and harmony or comfort, we are restless. In our relationships we have peace, harmony, and comfort as often as possible; when the chaos, imbalance, and discomfort outweigh the former, we are restless. If the relationship is filled with happiness and satisfaction, needs are being met, and good times are being had by all. It seems that the thought of infidelity vanishes.

Not so fast, sister. Many men and husbands cheat on their partners and still claim to have very happy marriages. Then how is it possible that a man will seek the company of another woman? Or how is it possible that a woman won't step out and spend time with another man? There are no guarantees that this cannot occur in the life span of your relationship. You do not have control over someone else.

Many men and husbands cheat on their partners and still claim to have very happy marriages.

If he cheats, it is he who has the character flaw; and if you cheat, you have that same flaw.

Is that what and who you want to be? Of course not. Is that who you thought he would turn out to be? Doubtful. But it happens, time and time again. There are at least two persons inside of us: the one we think we are, and the one we are. When it comes to being in a committed relationship and working with your partner, it's about taking the time to know the person they are, not the one they think they are. That's the intimacy you strive for.

♂ – DON

30 – Infidelity

Are you a cheater?

I think I once heard a comic, a man of course, say how great it would be to have sex with anybody and everybody we felt like on a daily basis. Similar to animals, we would not be bound to anyone. Picture a dog saying to another dog, "I know you want to do that French poodle across the street, so go ahead but then don't come back when you do!" I guess a man might feel some sort of elation at the thought of moving from bedroom to bedroom, and I guess you could live that sort of life. The problem with this, apart from contracting a disease or multiple diseases, is that you will never have the greatest sex of your life and you will also never be able to stay in one relationship over a lifetime.

As I am sure you have heard before, we live in a difficult time for marriages. Though times are always difficult because we are continuously evolving and culturally changing as a species, I refer to the specific difficulty that arises due to life spans. Never before have men and women lived so long. So if you are saying, "I do," in your twenties, you then have to plan on living with that person for another 50 years! That is a long time. Maybe 20-year-olds getting married today will live to 100, making it almost 80 years with the same woman. Some people get married with the idea that they can get divorced at any time, so it's no big deal. I say why get married if you are thinking like that. Just live together.

If you have gotten this far in the chapter and this far in the book, you have probably decided that you wish to have a lifelong relationship or at least you are contemplating it. You will need to stay faithful. Yes, as much as it might feel good to enjoy a little variety in your life, you will have to fantasize about it instead, because it is absolutely not right to cheat on your partner. Some people may say that it is the woman's responsibility to keep her man from straying, but I say it is your responsibility. You have control over your own actions and your own behavior. Stay true to your woman and only be with someone who will be true to you. More and more I hear about women cheating on their partners. Maybe it is more popular now that women are viewed as equals, or maybe it's just out in the open and less taboo. Women want an emotional connection, and if other men give them that attention, it becomes tempting. The emotional cheating a woman has with another man is still cheating and does not have to be physical. In some ways, it is worse.

I also want to mention that being unfaithful can be viewed in more than one way. Some people believe that infidelity refers to just the physical act, but what about the emotional or spiritual part? What if you were always physically faithful, but you were texting, phoning, and communicating with another woman? Wouldn't that be unfaithful? Anytime you get very close to another woman in any sense, you are being unfaithful. Friendship is certainly allowable between men and women, but I mean that it is not allowable when you go beyond friendship and give your heart to a woman other than your partner, even in a non-physical relationship. So even though you may rationalize this unfaithfulness by saying you are faithful physically, you are still not bound to your partner and therefore are not going to have the best sex of your life. That's right, I said you will never have the best sex of your life. Now if you have never experienced a relationship with a true partner, you wouldn't even know what I am talking about. Sure, you could have chandelier-swinging sex and that may feel very sexy and manly to you, but you will never have the kind of sex that you experience from being completely connected in every way to your partner. This means emotionally, mentally, spiritually, and physically.

> **Being unfaithful in any form means you will never have the kind of sex with your partner that you experience from being completely connected in every way.**

Every man has fantasies about being with other women, and that is normal. Acting on it is a very different thing. I have also found that when I am completely connected with my partner in every way, those fantasies go away. However, even if you are still having those fantasies, the only reasons you would have to act on them are immature in nature. If you fantasize about another woman and want to act on that fantasy, think about the reasons why you would pursue it. What would cause you to disrespect the woman you have committed to? Do you think it would just be fun? Would it be such a huge, stimulating event and feel so good that losing your partner wouldn't matter for the hour of happiness you would have? Wow, that must be some woman. I want you to know you can have even better sex with your partner. If you feel you cannot achieve that sexual greatness with your partner, you may have the wrong person. Sex is very important to men, and if you are not satisfied in this area, it could cause the downfall of your marriage. As divorce mediators, we find that the two biggest reasons for marriage failure are money and sex. Sex is also taboo, and the majority of people do not feel comfortable talking about this subject. You need to be honest with your inner man and know that sex is a biological need. Masturbation does not cut it. It may get rid of that initial need, but intimate sex with a physically, emotionally, spiritually, and mentally connected partner cannot be beat.

Honestly understand what it is inside of you that needs to have sex with another woman. The bottom line usually comes down to self-esteem.

Again, you have to honestly understand what it is inside of you that needs to have sex with another woman. The bottom line usually comes down to self-esteem. If you felt that you were manly enough and felt loved enough and connected enough, then having sex outside of your partnership would not matter. You would feel completely satisfied with your partner, and there would be no need for anything else. You also do not want to infect your partner with a disease you picked up somewhere else.

I will leave you with this final thought. If you are feeling that you want to have sex with other women, tell your partner. You can only do this successfully with a partner who has high self-esteem and is mature in her thinking. Otherwise, you will be dealing with a partner who never trusts you to go out, to look at another woman, or talk to other woman. As the saying goes, she will be on you like white on rice. However, if she is a mature woman with high self-esteem in both herself and your relationship, then telling her will stop you from acting on your thoughts. It will also enlist your partner to help you overcome the causes for your thinking. There is something missing in your life, and she can help you fill that gap. If she ignores your thinking or dismisses you, it's time to get a couples therapist involved or end the relationship.

♀ – DANA

31 – Arguing

Do You Swear Like a Sailor?

When I work with couples, one of the crucial components of their relationship is how they argue. If they say they don't argue, I don't believe them. No couple shares every opinion in common or agrees on everything. Maybe they don't argue; maybe they just disagree–agreeing to disagree; or maybe one is more dominant while the other is passive, which leads to a very unbalanced union. Countless times I have heard in my office, "You can't argue with her. It's her way or the highway," or "We don't argue. We never get the chance. As soon as he senses tension, he shuts down."

Couples have conflicts; conflicts are normal. The way you address conflict reflects a lot about both of you:

1. Much of how you argue has to do with how you grew up, the household and family that taught you what was and wasn't acceptable, and how you express your emotions when frustrated, desirous, needy, conflictual, and so on.

2. Sometimes, it has to do with the culture in which you were raised. Some cultures are known to be very expressive, loud, and boisterous, while other cultures may

have more restraint.

3.   Some households force members to repress, appease, or avoid any conflict, and now as adults, this continues. Or perhaps as an adult you realize that the pattern of conflict no longer works for you, and you have now found the freedom to express yourself differently. As a child you had to refrain from expressing anger, and now you see it as an injustice to your spirit. So now in your relationship you have given yourself permission to unleash those injustices and to let him and anyone else have a piece of your mind!

Whatever is your past or present conflict resolution trait, it impacts your relationship. It's important to resolve this and stay on track.

I have seen married couples come to me as a couple's therapist, with marriages that have to be re-worked in order to be saved. Most of the problems in their relationships were not only the results of poor communication, but poor communication topped with poor conflict management. If you learn how to argue fairly, then most likely, deep wounds and scars won't be a part of your history, and you could possibly sustain a happy, successful relationship. If you don't learn how to argue, discuss, and address each other fairly, then chances are that deep-seated wounds will mount up, causing hurts, bitterness, resentment, and scars that don't go away, therefore tarnishing what could have been a pure and beautiful union.

So make a point to learn how to share unpleasant feelings, wants, needs, disagreements, disappointments, and such in a constructive, mature, and productive manner. If you both can achieve this, then you both will have what you need individually and what the integrity of the relationship needs to be maintained, as well as the ability to maintain the integrity of the relationship, building it stronger and stronger to a solid union, rather than chipping away at it like a decayed wisdom tooth.

Hopefully, you are in a relationship with someone who has a set of core values and principals, as you have yourself. Equal sharing of these core values, principals, beliefs, wants, and needs is required in order to meet a goal, whether it concerns raising your children or who is going to take out the garbage. Unequal sharing of those characteristics and conflict can arise from a minor disagreement. This can range from conflict about you going out with friends on Friday after work or meeting them for brunch on Sunday; to disagreement when one who has lost their employment wants to relax on unemployment benefits but their partner feels that immediate efforts to search and secure a job is the priority.

The best way you are going to secure your relationship is to learn how to fight fairly. If you came from a family that argued, screamed and yelled, and said hurtful things, then you may want to consider a new way. If you came from a family who didn't say anything and deployed the silent treatment or maintained a tense environment without anyone ever really addressing the problem, then you may want to change that. Even if you are somewhere in the middle, maybe wielding sarcasm, bullying, hostility, temporary shutouts, withholding of affection as punishment, whining, pouting, sulking, manipulating, spitefulness, or cutting remarks—do any of these look familiar?—you may also reconsider a better approach.

The best way you are going to secure your relationship is to learn how to fight fairly.

Maybe it's just on his end that corrections need to be made. Is that the case? You still need to read this because, if he is arguing with you, it's still your action or reaction that forms the other side of the disagreement.

The first thing you want to rely on is the **"Speaker, Listener"** concept. This means that when she speaks her point within a reasonable time frame, he listens, and vice versa. The time frame is a huge part of this. You cannot, as the Speaker, drone on and on, repeating what you have said over and over again as though he didn't hear you the first five times. The Listener will verify that he heard you by repeating what you said. You can even ask for that reiteration after you state your case, saying, "What is it that you just heard me say?"

The problem is usually that, while you're talking, the Listener is thinking about what he is going to say because he is concerned he may forget it, never hearing you at all. You want to eliminate that. Anxiety also prevents the Listener from hearing you. This applies to both of you, and when he speaks and it's your turn to listen, you may notice this very truth yourself.

In order to eliminate this, it's OK to write your thoughts on a scrap of paper. However, if you are truly engaged in

> **Use the "Speaker, Listener" concept: This means that when she speaks her point within a reasonable time frame, the other listens. The Listener will verify that he heard her by repeating what she said. Take care that neither of you occupy your minds with what you're going to say while the other is speaking. The goal is to solve the problem, not win the fight.**

the discussion and points of view are being shared for the purpose of resolution, then it won't matter if you forget some clever little comment, fail to bring up a good example of what he does wrong, or overlook a criticism because the greater good is to solve the problem, not prove who the champion prize fighter is.

Stay on topic; don't drag in the past; don't call each other names; don't say something you don't mean. Sometimes one feels the need to be dramatic. Stop. Don't be so dramatic; take an acting class if you need center stage. Be honest. Don't assume that he is going to say something or act a certain way; you don't want to typecast your partner. Remember, he is still your man, and you love him. You don't want to humiliate him. Be willing to hear his side; respect and honor his perspective even if you don't agree; and try to compromise. A relationship that is healthy brings both points of view to the table.

You will solve the problem using these techniques, and the more civil and logical the process, the better for the identity of your relationship. You don't want to be known as the "Bickerings" next door."

32 – Arguing

Do you ever win an argument?

Do you ever wonder what is fair when arguing with your partner? Do you ever wonder if you should push back or accept her yelling as venting? There need to be boundaries when arguing with your partner. If you and your partner are consistently arguing and yelling at each other, then you should take a good, hard, honest look and determine whether the two of you just like to argue for the sake of arguing or if you are really trying to help your partner understand your perspective. However, arguing for the sake of arguing will never result in a productive end or a resolution.

First, you need to understand a couple of things. Are you or your partner the one who usually starts the argument? When you argue, does each of you just want to win for the sake of winning, or do you actually care if you understand what the other one is saying? Do you insult and curse at each other? Do you throw objects? Will you never stop arguing until there is some sort of resolution, sometimes arguing about the same thing over days and maybe weeks at a time?

Once you honestly answer these questions, you may know what needs to change. If after reading them you still don't know how to respond to these questions, then think about the questions when you are in the middle of the argument. Barking at each other until one side gets tired of barking never solves anything, except for the benefit of feeling good about arguing, if that's what you are looking for. Think about when you feel good. Do you feel good when she gives in? Do you feel good even if there is no resolution except that the two of you acknowledge you are different? You need to understand each other because it can cause serious issues down the line if neither one of you is listening to the other. You have to understand each one of your motives during the arguments, and the motive could be different at different times. Once you understand your partner's and your motives, you can proceed. If you still don't know, then you need to keep talking about it with your partner until you do.

After you correct your motive for arguing, you can easily fall into the trap of arguing the way you did before, but it is important to keep on track and make a new habit for arguing.

Now that you have an understanding of the motive for each of you, you can make some changes if the motive is incorrect or does not feel right. It will feel uncomfortable because you can easily fall into the trap of arguing the way you did before, but it is important to keep on track and make a new habit for arguing. You will also need to keep each other in check. The first thing you will need to do is set up some rules and boundaries:

- Neither one of you can talk over the other person. Only one person is allowed to talk at a time. Some people have kept this in check by having a talking stick that is passed back and forth. A talking stick is something you hold, maybe a spatula or whatever you have, and only the person with this stick is able to speak.

- Next is to have no name-calling. If you can't seem to keep this in check, then each of you puts a dollar in a jar every time you insult the other person, and you have to apologize to the other party if you stoop to insults. You are not allowed to generalize about men or women. This takes away from the argument at hand and does not help you come to a resolution.

- You are not allowed to switch topics. Discuss one topic at a time. Only talk about that one topic until you either come to a resolution or make a joint decision that you agree to disagree on the subject and will never come to a resolution.

- You may have to put a time limit on the discussion, and if you find that tempers are starting to flair, each of you should take a breath and then start up again. It's OK as long as you each respect the other person's feelings about the subject and you don't get angry at them for having their own opinion. You may feel that they are just not listening to you, but if you cannot communicate your understanding, then it is best to drop it and maybe pick up again when you have the words to discuss, or have thought about, your own perspective.

- Do not bring anybody else into the discussion. This only complicates things and shows the other person you do not feel strong enough to have the discussion on your own. The only time this would not be true is if you had an unbiased third party involved to mediate the discussion. A mediator will listen to both sides, help you with the communication between those sides, and maybe help you see a third side that could be a solution for both of you. As divorce and family mediators, this is what we do because emotions get so strong and convolute thinking. You need someone to look at the facts and help you reach a decision.

- If you find that your partner is struggling with the subject, then help her out. Give her the words. Even if it does not help you progress your point of view, you want to make sure you truly understand her perspective. A lot of times, women get caught up in their emotions and may not be able to logically think through a subject. This is because their left and right brains are more connected than a man's. A man is able to separate logic from emotion because his brain does not have the same connections as a woman's. Help her think through the message she is trying to convey.

- Never bring up the past. You need to stay on one subject and only on the current events. Bringing up subjects from the past convolutes the present situation, and if you feel like you keep doing this, it may be because of your ego. Leave your ego at the door, and be prepared to give in to your partner's understanding. There has to be a give and take on both sides. Allow your partner the time to think about what you said, and also allow her to formulate her thoughts and ideas based on your argument and ideas. You each may need to take a breather just to help each of you take in the discussion and internalize it. It is OK to take a breather and pick up where you left off.

- Lastly, you cannot have a huge discussion about every little thing in the relationship. Pick and choose the battles and know when to end them. It is not good to just argue for argument's sake.

The last thought I will leave with you is if one of you is arguing by yelling, insulting, cursing, generalizing, or belittling the other person, then this is the ego wanting to argue for the sake of arguing. You need to put an end to this immediately. If your partner is doing this, then you need your partner to take a breath. Explain to her how you are feeling. Make sure you tell her how you are feeling instead of what she is doing. She can't argue with you about your feelings—even though women can argue about anything—but you can remind her that she needs to honor the way you feel. It gives you power that you need to protect yourself in your relationship. Yes, she loves you, but only you really know how you feel inside.

> **If one of you is arguing by yelling, insulting, cursing, generalizing, or belittling the other person, then this is the ego wanting to argue for the sake of arguing.**

♀ – DANA

33 – Self-Esteem

How do you measure self-worth?

As you may have heard, when a couple joins together it should look like two independent individuals rather than half a person each. As I'm sure you have been told, a healthy relationship rests on the concept that you need to be a whole person first.

This "whole" includes having self-esteem. Without a healthy level of self-reflection to assess your self-worth, you may not know exactly how you measure up. Self-worth is valuing yourself with respect and a favorable opinion. If you don't value yourself, no one else will, and this lack of knowledge can prohibit you from having a long-lasting, loving relationship.

Women who love and love to give without expecting to receive have a lower level of self-esteem. If you are the kind of woman in the relationship who offers much of themselves, their energy, time, and effort and doesn't ask their partner to give back equal amounts of his time, energy, and effort, you may be in an unbalanced partnership and will be exploited. As the old saying goes, "Your kindness is taken as weakness." So be careful and assess your self-worth.

Self-esteem is developed in your early childhood, mostly sourcing from parents, family, and friends with

whom you are in close relationship. Their responses to
you matter. If you grew up with positive role models who
exhibited their own self-worth and were praised, while your
accomplishments were recognized as well, then chances are
very good that you have a healthy level of self-esteem. If
you were raised in a household that didn't take notice of
your accomplishments or that focused more on negative
behaviors since nothing you did was good enough, chances
are your self-esteem level was compromised. The problem is
that, as an adult, it is difficult to improve
self-worth a great deal. Childhood
leaves a permanent imprint upon us,
although this is not to say we cannot
improve and grow and develop
ourselves fully. Luckily we can, and
if you feel your relationship may be
or will be sabotaged because of low
self-esteem issues, then you really
owe it to yourself to look for ways to
improve it. The caveat is that you may
not recognize this state, due to the very
nature of your low self-esteem. So let's take
a look at ways in which you might recognize within yourself
or your partner the need to improve self-worth.

> **It is difficult as an adult, but luckily we can improve self-worth even though negative childhood programming leaves a permanent imprint upon us.**

For the woman who envisions a man sweeping them
off their feet, rescuing them, or taking care of them, this
relates to the father figure in their life. If you think that
your father saved you as a child—maybe he did; maybe he
didn't—it becomes the concept of idealizing him as perfect.
Your partner would have to maintain or achieve this
perfection, which is not possible. Your recurring need to
feel that important sense of being saved develops in order
for you to overcome the regret, in your eyes, that it was

your fault and that you weren't worth saving. This overflows into a sabotage of the relationship, which consists of testing your partner due to your own possible insecurities of feeling unlovable. Testing your partner in various ways or constantly asking, "Do you love me?" is a sign that you are not convinced that this man or any man can truly love you.

Are you manipulatively applying your sexual or physical powers based on a need for financial security? This is deceptive plotting and unacceptable to yourself and partner. Wrapping yourself up with a partner for the sake of security out of a sense of low self-esteem avoids showing your partner who you really are. Perhaps there are areas of yourself that you are hiding. Using your good looks or sexual talents to hold on or lure your partner to take care of you will only backfire later on when either you or he can no longer sustain the façade.

Be aware that your low self-esteem has been a difficult cross to bear, and you have been constantly working hard to gain traction with it. No one really enjoys feeling bad about themselves. If you question whether your self-worth has impacted your relationship and feelings of insecurity continually seep into arguments; or if you lack trust in your partner or how he feels abut you, then please confide in a professional. Address these insecurities and assess where the level of self-worth measures up for you. Healthy, high self-esteem is our human right. If for some reason you did not get your entitled dose, then know that there is plenty waiting for you and you need to work on getting what's rightfully yours. A healthy self is a happy self, filled with a positive attitude toward yourself and your partner.

♂ – DON

34 – Self-Esteem

Do you feel like a rock star?

Self-esteem is a difficult matter because people mask such issues in many ways. Most of the time, people do not even realize they have self-esteem problems. You could have high self-esteem in all areas of your life and still have low self-esteem in your relationship. This happens for many different reasons and can negatively impact all aspects of your relationship. It can affect how you argue, how you overcome hurdles, how much trust you have, and can mask itself in many different ways. A relationship cannot really

> **A relationship cannot really be healthy if one partner has low self-esteem.**

be healthy if one partner has low self-esteem. If self-esteem is low, you will not trust your partner. For example, if you have low self-esteem and your partner is talking with another guy, it will really bother you, and it may bother you for days, weeks, and even months in some cases. It is extremely important for you to discuss this with your partner. Likewise, if your partner feels this way when you talk to other girls, she needs to tell you how this makes her feel. Insecurity is usually high in a relationship at the start and decreases over time as the trust and comfort builds up. You do not know each other at first, and trust should build over time, growing as your partnership grows. However, some people never get out of that low level of self-esteem and may need individual therapy to help them do so. Most of the time, this self-esteem is created within the person, and therefore, that person needs to be the one to make some adjustments to improve it. Yes, there are some people who cannot be trusted. That does not necessarily mean there is a self-esteem issue, but there maybe an issue with your partner.

When arguing, low self-esteem will cause you to argue in ways that are detrimental to the relationship and will most likely tear it apart. If your partner has low self-esteem and is insulting you, bringing up the past, and never addressing the issue at hand when you argue, it is most likely because she doesn't feel good about herself in the relationship. She is either unwilling to discuss that issue, or she may not even know where those feelings are coming from. It is up to you to point this out in the right way. If you feel like you are always walking on eggshells and a fight could break out at any minute, then low self-esteem is most likely the culprit. She is unhappy with the lack of connection between the two of you, is not feeling the closeness of a true healthy relationship, and is having trouble getting intimate.

You will want to know the real level of her sex libido, not one prompted by low self-esteem, because if her low self-esteem improves over time, you might find that she actually has a really low libido and you might never get enough sex.

You also may find that your partner wants to have sex a lot because she wants to hold on to you and knows sex is important to you. Yes, this may feel really good at first because she wants to have sex, but she is doing it for the wrong reasons. You might not even care, but remember, it is better when the sex comes from a solid relationship. You also want to know the real level of her sex libido because, if it is coming from low self-esteem and her self-esteem improves over time, you might find that she actually has a really low libido, and then you will never get enough sex. Find out now.

If your partner has good self-esteem in your relationship, it will also be a lot easier for her to overcome relationship hurdles, and it will not feel like her world is falling apart every time you have a fight. With low self-esteem comes constant questioning of your love, questioning about your behavior, questions about your night out with the guys and in everything that you do. This can be the basis for failure in your relationship. She may need constant validation of your love because she will never feel good about it.

If both of you have high self-esteem in the relationship, it can help you build a great, healthy connection. You will each feel independent, knowing it is OK to be apart. You don't have to worry because you fully trust your partner, you argue like mature adults, and you encourage and support each other when overcoming hurdles. People with good self-esteem are extremely attractive.

Lastly, be sure that your partner is not coming from a place of ego. Your partner's ego can push you away, and your ego could push your partner away. Ego sometimes comes up when we are afraid to be vulnerable. However, our egos have to be put aside before we can be in a truly healthy relationship.

♀ – DANA

35 – Domestic Violence

How will you know this is unhealthy?

In your relationship, you may have felt possessed, perhaps criticized or put down, and when you brought this up to your partner, he told you that you were too sensitive. In some relationships, we might misinterpret what is actually unhealthy love for romantic love. Knowing your partner and understanding how he loves is vitally important. He may say he loves you, professing love whole-heartedly, but he himself is not aware of his inability to love another.

Abusive relationships come in a variety of disguises. He does not have to be physically aggressive toward you; he may not even be a screamer. But you may be in an abusive domestic relationship, also known as intimate partner violence.

Take a look at the following behaviors. Have you noticed evidence of these behaviors, to any degree?

- He is always angry at someone or something.

- He doesn't listen to you or show interest in your opinions.

- He blames all arguments or problems on you.

- He lies to you, doesn't show up for dates, or maybe disappears for days.

- He has taken your money or taken advantage of you in other ways.

- He tries to isolate you and control whom you see or where you go.

- He has mood swings: one minute you are wonderful and the next minute he rips you apart.

These are just a few signs. There are more physical and violent behaviors, and if he has pushed you or in any way shoved you, consider that also as abusive. Have you been afraid to break up with him? Have you felt tied down or feel like you have to check in with him? Do you ever tell yourself that if you could make him happy everything would be all right? These are signs that the relationship hinges on power. Therefore the relationship is an unhealthy one, and most times it gets worse. Only the abuser can stop it; there is nothing the victim can do. It is the abuser's problem.

Oftentimes women really fall for the abuser and then stay with him because of a compassion they feel for him. He may have come from **Oftentimes women really fall for the abuser and then stay with him because of a compassion they feel for him.** an abusive childhood, and now it's you who will make him feel loved and cared for. Unfortunately, it doesn't work like this. Abusers and batterers require professional help in learning how to control their behavior, while at the same time understanding and dealing with the trauma that has caused them this need for control over others.

Did you know that the majority of domestic violence victims are women? There are men who are also victims, and this is not a one-sided problem. Women have abusive behaviors as well and have seriously injured or killed their male partners. Statistics show up mostly for women as victims, but know that it is a concern for both men and women.

According to the Domestic Violence Statistics & Facts report issued by Safe Horizon, the largest victims' services agency in the U.S.:

- Each year approximately 2 million women suffer non-fatal but serious violence at the hands of their current or former intimate partners.

- Approximately half of abused women are battered during pregnancy. Over 75% of violent children have witnessed violence between their parents.

- When it comes to intimate partner abuse, one in four women will experience domestic violence during her lifetime. Women experience more than 4 million physical assaults and rapes because of their partners, and men are victims of nearly 3 million physical assaults.

- Women are more likely to be killed by an intimate partner than men. Women of ages 20 to 24 are at greatest risk of becoming victims.

- Children who grew up in violent homes are more likely to become abusers or victims. It's important to talk to your partner about his childhood home and ask if there was any level of violence. Households may not always exhibit violence and terror, yet power and control in the home was prevalent.

If you believe that this cannot happen to you or your friends and family, you are wrong. Abuse can happen regardless of gender, race, ethnicity, sexual orientation, level of education, income, or other factors. Safe Horizon reports that victims can be any age.

Psychological and emotional abuse can take the form of name-calling, humiliation, constant criticism, or harming the victim's relationship with his or her children. This can also be known as parent alienation. Psychological abuse of a victim occurs for a length of time and even for the duration of the relationship. The worst part of it is that the longer the relationship lasts, the more psychological damage is done.

The longer the relationship lasts, the more psychological damage is done, and the victim accepts as truth the derogatory barbs he hurls at her.

For example, when the controller uses his power to intimidate and isolate, the victim's self-esteem decreases. Over time, as the psychological games, coercion, and lying continue, the victim accepts as truth those derogatory barbs he hurls at her. He may call her crazy, making her doubt herself and her choices; this results in her depending more on him. He may tell her she is unattractive, or she looks stupid in an outfit, making her believe that she is ugly, unappealing, and undesirable to anyone else—therefore she won't leave him. If she ever stands up for herself, telling him off, he only minimizes her complaint. He may deny what he just said to her, or blame her for making him say whatever negative insult it was. He may even laugh in her face.

As the victim lives under these conditions for a period of time, it becomes more difficult to leave. Most times he has isolated her from forming outside relationships with friends or coworkers. If she shows any interest in having a social connection, he may make her feel guilty about leaving him to spend time with friends. If there are children, he may discourage her from going out because "the children need her more than her friends do." If she forms any friendships, he will find fault with them, eventually causing her to distance herself from them. She again will find herself home and alone, serving him, and he likes it this way. If she tries to form friendships, he makes it so difficult with his obstacles or insults, or sometimes he tells her that her friend is not trustworthy and is just using her. She then gives up trying to form any outside relationships as she is too sick of trying.

Women who find themselves in these relationships usually gravitate toward them due to familiarity and family of origin. Maybe one parent held a position of power and control, thus impressing upon a victim that this is a normal dynamic of relationship, keeping this victim in a similar powerless position in their own relationship. Victims also find themselves in powerless positions due to low self-esteem. Victims tend to stay in abusive relationships for various other reasons, like economic dependence, fear of retaliation, fear of emotional damage to the children, or maybe losing custody. Social isolation can leave the victim wondering whom they would turn to since there are no longer friends or family to rely upon. Or perhaps the victim just doesn't know there are alternatives and that life can improve a great deal, if they just took that first step.

Guilt can also play a role. The victim either believes it is their fault or that the abuser isn't going to be OK alone, and that to end the relationship may be worse. The victim can become entrapped by pity for the abuser and the desire for nothing to happen. Sometimes a victim can rationalize staying and say, "This is an illness and he needs help; I can't leave him."

A learned pattern of "helplessness" in the family history can be repeated and keep a victim powerless. The worst truth about the victim in an abusive relationship—either verbally, emotionally, or physically abusive—is that she or he is in denial. In asking yourself if you are a victim or maybe a perpetrator, see if the following resonate for you. Is/are there:

- criticism?

- overprotective behavior, jealousy?

- threats of hurting loved ones, animals, children, family, friends?

- sudden bursts of anger?

- destruction of personal property, throwing things?

- use of intimidation?

- prevention of freedom to be with friends or to go out shopping, walking, to the gym, etc.?

- forced sex?

- humiliation, embarrassment?

When you review the above list, are there any of the conditions that appear in your relationship? If so, then talk to a professional and get the resources and assistance you need. This behavior does not stop on its own.

Severe cases exist in which the abuser becomes physically abusive. Yet rarely does anyone outside the home know about it. He is able to conceal his rage and target only her, even to the point of hiding it from the children. She is alone, and although he may hit her and leave marks, no one believes her because no one sees it happening. The abuser is usually very clever and charming, making it even more unbelievable that he is violent and controlling behind closed doors. He will also threaten her if she does tell anyone. He may say she will ruin his career, they will be out on the street or lose everything, and their lifestyle will disappear. The children will resent her, and their demise will be all of her fault.

It almost seems impossible to remove herself from this marriage. It is almost impossible to divorce someone like him, because most abusers are narcissists. If the divorce includes dividing up assets, he never agrees. He would rather burn the house down than be ordered to hand over belongings that he believes belong entirely up to him, and this includes the children.

When it comes to sexual control, the humiliation is worse. Sex is degrading to the victim; she is objectified; and sex is only for his pleasure. The abuser, as a narcissist, also engages in sex as a means of power and believes that he is the best lover. He sets his mind to thinking that she should be awed and grateful. Sex usually takes place whenever he decides it should, but then he complains that she never initiates it. He complains of feeling deprived and that she needs to make more of an effort to please him. Women in these scenarios lack the desire of romance. Her initiation of sex with her partner is mostly to keep him happy, in fear of the alternative. She will try to force herself to initiate by affection or by doing something kind and generous that he likes so he might take the hint that she is interested in him. But, as an intention to still keep her under his thumb, he will reject her advances and humiliate her even more. She may feel temporary relief that she just got a free pass out of the bedroom, but not for long; most of the time, before the night is over, he takes what he wants. And the cycle continues.

One of the key components to domestic violence is the cycle of abuse. You may have heard of the "honeymoon" phase. This is after the abuse has escalated—whether it was an explosive rage, hitting, or some other explosive episode–when the victim has received the torment and the abuser has calmed down. He may apologize and express remorse, promising he won't ever do this again; or admitting he needs help and will seek help; or expressing such regret that he even convinces himself that he is in the wrong. This is the phase that sucks the victim back in. But don't be fooled; the cycle continues. It may be days or weeks, but unless professional intervention has begun, the abuse will return. And around and around it goes.

One of the key components to domestic violence is the "honeymoon" phase in the cycle of abuse.

The victim is not sure exactly what triggers him or when he gets triggered. Sometimes it is random; sometimes it is apparent. But when the abuser wants to lash out, he will lash out because he feels entitled to his rage. He tells himself he is justified.

Who is the abuser? Why is he so controlling? There are reasons from early childhood from which the abuser has learned this behavior.

Identifying the abuser isn't always easy since his distinguishing behavior is not detectable in the early stages of the relationship. The early signs may be that he has "fallen head over heels in love," and it was "love at first sight." He may say he has never been in love like this before; he may propose marriage within six months. Be careful. This may all seem flattering and intensely romantic, but unfortunately it is not real. It is only their way of manipulating and controlling your future. Once he is more comfortable, he will let down his guard. Jealousy is usually another sign. Certain signs of possessiveness may be insecurity, however jealously becomes a big concern when it turns into obsession.

Learning more about his childhood is essential. Did

he experience abuse or neglect growing up? If he can talk about his childhood trauma, with insight and reflection, perhaps the relationship has the potential for healthy self-awareness and prevention of generational abuse. However, if he uses this poor upbringing as an excuse for his resentment or sense of entitlement, then you may consider this relationship as a dangerous one. This entitlement or belief that he deserves special treatment gives him this unjust sense of superiority. When you disappoint him or you don't give him what he asks for, he doesn't know how to manage this and sees it as neglect, abandonment, or disrespect. His behavior shows up as having been injured, that life is unjust and unfair. He will not back down until he gets what he believes he deserves. If you stay with him, you will notice that what was once his intent to please you has now shifted to what pleases him—he is more important.

Know that this is an unhealthy love and not really love at all. Why would you stay in an abusive relationship? Fear or pity that he will be distraught or suicidal if you leave him could arise. You may believe that abuse is normal; perhaps you grew up in an abusive home yourself. Perhaps you may be embarrassed to admit that you loved this man and thought he was the greatest catch in all the land, but now the truth is that you were fooled. Maybe you suffer from low self-esteem, and sadly, the worst reason is that you actually believe he will change.

This is an unhealthy love and not really love at all.

The most important thing you can do for yourself is to trust your instincts. If you cannot rely on that, then keep your friends and family close and trust their feedback. His behavior may not be as apparent to them as he will conceal it. But over time, loved ones will notice the change in you. They will notice how you may be less visible; you may check in with him more often as if needing permission; you may seem depressed, hypervigilant, and not your happy self. If someone is telling you that they see something different and it's not good, then listen to them. Confide in someone who will give you honest feedback, and get the help you need to remove yourself from the situation.

♂ – DON

36 – Domestic Violence

Have you been verbally neutered?

From a man's perspective, domestic violence is an extremely sensitive subject. It is acutely difficult for a man to claim he is being abused by a woman because he is ridiculed for alleging such a thing. No one usually believes him unless there are marks. For this reason, men do not want to speak up when they are abused. Abuse can be physical or verbal. In some cases, the verbal abuse can have more long-lasting effects than the physical abuse.

Studies have shown that men have almost the same rate of abuse as women. Almost all funding for domestic violence victims are directed to women and not men. For example, check out VAWA (Violence Against Women's Act). Even though the rate of abuse is virtually the same between men's abuse of women and women's abuse of men, according to the CDC, the funding from the federal government is directed to women.

A man is ridiculed for alleging abuse by a woman and is taught to "shut up and take it like a man."

It is not easy for a man to claim domestic violence because most have been brought up to "shut up and take it like a man," and they also have been told it is wrong for a man to cry. So what should a man do?

SPEAK UP! If you don't speak up about it, then you will continue the cycle of abuse. If you have any children, your children will continue the cycle of not speaking up. So even if you do not care about yourself or what is happening to you, do it for the sake of your children or other men.

It is easy to know if you are physically abused, and studies have shown that women use weapons when physically abusing men almost 90% of the time. However, how do you know when you are verbally abused? How do you know when enough is enough, and what can you do if you are consistently abused verbally? Signs of verbal abuse consist of constant criticism, yelling and screaming on a regular basis, always being blamed, insults, and threatening language. In other words, if your partner says things regularly that don't feel good, it is verbal abuse. You need to act like a man, speak up, and tell her how you're feeling. Don't hold it in because the feelings you are disguising or holding back will affect your health, mental and physical. It may not come out right away, but at some point it will.

On another note, you should know that women sometimes use a false claim of domestic violence as an excuse in family court to gain custody of the children and get the father thrown out of the house. It is a tactic that has been used for years. I do not condone domestic violence at all, but when someone is falsely and purposefully accused of doing something, to be used as a tool against them, it is seriously wrong. I know you think your partner would never falsely accuse you, but there are many men today that also thought the same thing about their partner before it happened to them. Your partner can literally go down to family court, even if there are no children, get an order of protection against you, and have you thrown out of the house that same day. Unbelievable, I know, but true. It sometimes takes months to get back into the house, and you probably won't be able to see your children at all for that whole time, unless you are allowed supervised visitation.

After you have recognized that your partner is verbally abusing you or has physically abused you multiple times and won't get the help or doesn't recognize that there is a problem, it is time to run. Run as fast as you can and don't look back!

37 – Is it Time?

How will you know this is unhealthy?

Now that each of you have read through this book that Don and I slaved over just to save you from a life of marriage misery, I can only hope that your appreciation of a real relationship with your partner has deepened and your heart has expanded.

I hope you have found the one with whom you want to do all this great work. As you carefully prepare for the marital ceremony and the thoughts run through your head—like "Is this the guy for me?"—think about the fact that you have read this book. As a result, you have explored a multitude of behaviors with him while interacting in multiple ways: with him and his family; in your relationship with him and his relationship with your family; with individual friends, collective friends, new friends, old friends, the neighbors, the waiter, etc. You also feel that in this amount of time, many experiences have tested and revealed your staying power.

Those problem areas that caused tension, or conflict, or misunderstanding were addressed and drawn to an equitable resolution. You also have been honest and have accepted who he is today while accepting the idea of his continuing growth and allowing that this growth may be in areas that you wouldn't necessarily think of as a priority. But you remember that this is the area he chooses to develop, and you allow him to explore his own path, just as you are entitled to choose your path, as long as both paths lead to a healthy, positive, fulfilling life together.

There are "love at first sights," "happily ever afters," "re-united after the wars," "soul mates," "high school sweethearts," and many more magical storybook testimonies that inspire us, from couples who have stayed together and proudly share their stories as successful ones. We hopeless romantics all want to believe that true love exists.

We hopeless romantics all want to believe that true love exists. This book was not written to discourage but rather to prepare and make marriage work.

Let us not forget that the idea of marriage originated as a financial arrangement between two families; the young couple was given land and a dowry to begin their lives and prosper. Love was rarely the impetus to contract for marriage. The first grand wedding was planned by Queen Victoria, and the white dress was chosen for the convenience of cleaning white more easily than colored fabric, not because it was virginal.

Marriage contracts are financial agreements, and it should not shock you to know then that a divorce is a lawsuit to break the contract.

So do we marry for financial security? Do we marry for love? Going back to the earlier chapter, "Marriage, is this really what you want?" and having read from there to here, perhaps you are more aware of who you are in the game of matrimony. Most of you who have read this book will still marry. That's wonderful since this book was not written to discourage but rather to prepare and make marriage work.

We as mediators will lose your business, and that's fine as long as you both stay true to each other, raise great kids, and live well by your rules. We know that many couples will marry anyway, despite knowing they are ill fit, and will come to us to separate. We won't sit there on our high horses and say, "WE TOLD YOU SO." We will welcome their business, make sure their separation is amicable and fair, and with some counseling, prepare them for healing, assessing, and moving on.

If you are now on the fence and have canceled the check to the caterer, then let's explore what has caused your ambivalence. Fear? Good. Caution and deliberation are key components to purposeful decisions. The idea here is to think about the person to whom you are making a commitment. Do you love this person enough that you can live together honestly, openly, vulnerably, compassionately, sacrificially, parentally, ambitiously, creatively, humorously, financially, equitably, sexually, intimately, medically, familially, and through the good days and bad?

How do you know? You don't. You might as well be honest right now, at the beginning, before you lie to yourself. You do not know if you will live "happily ever after," or if this person is your "soul mate." The truth is, you cannot possibly know; most couples love each other and hope for the best. And some go into marriage with the attitude that if it doesn't work out, call a mediator and dissolve it.

Will you do the work necessary to keep love alive?

The only thing you need to know and worry about is, will you do the work necessary to keep love alive?

Here comes the bride . . . .

38 – Is It Time?

Is it I DO *or* I DON'T?

So you have come to this point in your relationship, and now you feel really comfortable with the one you have chosen and are ready to take the plunge. Have you thought about everything? And I don't mean the flowers, band, photographer, etc. What I mean is, do you know whom you are marrying and have you thought about "the things" you need to work on as a couple? You say you don't know what I am talking about? Well, you need to understand the dynamics of your relationship. Based on the guidance written in this book, have you put it all together and do you understand what work you have to do? Every relationship has the possibility of succeeding if you are prepared to do the work. Some people say there is no work if you really love each other. Well, some people do really love each other, yet after time, the relationship fails. There are several different reasons for this, and though you could say that it would never happen to you, I also say: no pain, no gain. That's true in bodybuilding and true in mind and soul as well. In order for a muscle to grow, you have to stretch it to its limits

Every relationship has the possibility of succeeding if you are prepared to do the work.

until it develops little tears. Those tears then heal, and you have a bigger, stronger muscle. The same is true with a relationship, your mind, and your spiritual self. Those things may not matter to you now, but they may matter in the future when you are trying to deal with the negative side of divorce.

Just so you are aware, she is expecting you to change. Yes, she is EXPECTING you to change. She has already sized you up, she knows the things she is uncomfortable with, and she is ready to initiate some changes in you as soon as you and she say, "I do." That's when she gets to work. The changes may include getting rid of those friends of yours. Now you say, "No way; my friends and I enjoy watching the football game on Sundays." Well, you can forget about those football games; she will have a special day planned with her parents. You may think you have a say in this, but just wait until after the marriage. She will be very convincing. This is just one thing that may happen after marriage, and it may not be the exact thing she wants to change at all. But be very clear—she wants to change something in you. And if you are already planning the wedding, just know she is planning the changes that she wants in you.

The unfortunate thing about marriage is that expectations are created, and if those expectations are not then met, you and she are upset, and the relationship starts to sour. You may not even know that you have expectations, but they are there. Also, make sure your expectations are your own expectations and are not formulated from someone else's. These expectations become your needs and wants, and it is extremely important to understand yours and those of your future spouse. You need to discuss these before the marriage, just to set the record straight and know if there will be work involved or if your partner has expectations you know you cannot meet. Don't lie about how you are feeling or what you think she expects. Don't be so quick to say YES to whatever is asked of you, in the hopes that you can conquer the world with her by your side. You may get everything you want, but then again, there may be things that don't exactly go right, and that's when you could be in for the surprise of your life: "I WANT A DIVORCE." It never feels good to hear those words; or at that point, she may be saying just what you are feeling. Why let it get to that point? Do the work now and make your lives great.

Don't lie about how you are feeling or what you think she expects. Discuss these before the marriage. Do the work now and make your lives great.

Don't you think you would be happy if all of your needs and wants were being met? Of course you would. That's why it is so important for you to know yourself and know your partner. It's important to know their values, beliefs, and role in the marriage or relationship. Instead of going to a movie, how about talking about each other and getting to know her. It's fun to have a collective experience, but it doesn't get you any closer to your goal of knowing if this is the right person for you. If you are not looking for a long-term relationship, then it is important to know that as well, and if that really is the case, not to kid yourself.

Of course you could listen to your family and friends about marriage, and everyone will have their own ideas, but the thing that they may not tell you is that your relationship and your marriage are individual and unique journeys. What may be right for them is not right for you. So be prepared for the wrong advice from anybody and everybody. Listen with a discerning ear. Understand why they are saying what they are saying and how it applies to you. Be careful not to allow yourself to be easily influenced. When people speak, they sound so rational, how could you not follow their advice? However like I said before, marriages and relationships are individual journeys. You may be asking yourself, "If I am in a relationship, how can this be an individual journey?" The answer is simple: because your expectations, your needs, your wants, and how you behave are all individual. Yet in your marriage and relationship, you will want to work on individual as well as team goals. Yes, marriage should be a team effort and a partnership too.

When picking a partner, everyone usually starts by dating, unless your parents select your partner in an arranged marriage. In arranged marriages, you may have a better chance at success because your parents probably know you better than you do and know what's right for you. They also do not make the choice out of emotions. For the parents, the choice is logical. Love can be built over time, similar to when people grow together. You do not find a soul mate. You find someone who has potential to be a soul mate, and over time, if you do the work, you can have that soul mate. In the beginning, people sometimes mistake lust for love, but most cannot tell the difference between the two.

Here is another little tidbit for you. You don't want her to change, and she is perfect just the way she is. However, as soon as you are married, things will start changing: she WILL change. You really don't know what that change will be until after you are married. She may not be that easy-going, sweet girl that you knew when you proposed. She may go into control mode. Nothing you do is right. How do you think that will feel? Not good? Now you may be thinking that that's not the harmonious nature of the agreement you both entered into. Meanwhile, she is thinking to herself that you don't care if she transforms into her alter ego. She is now your wife, and she now has the power to do as she pleases with you and the relationship. Don't give in to that and make sure you provide your input. Don't let her run the show because you would be setting a lasting precedent that would make you feel like less of a man. You should both feel you have a say in the relationship, not just her.

> **She is perfect just the way she is. However, as soon as you are married, she WILL change. She may go into control mode. Don't give in to that and make sure you provide your input. You should both feel you have a say in the relationship.**

You run the biggest risk by marrying in your twenties. As you get older, you reduce the risk because you are maturing and learning more about yourself and your partner as well. This is why it is important to really know the strengths and weaknesses of the person you are marrying. You will be a team, and you are making a lifetime commitment. Make sure you have someone on your side who can help you be the best you can be. In addition, you should be able to help your partner be the best she can be as well.

When a relationship is in the beginning stages, you feel really great. Everyone is on their best behavior because they want to impress. Everybody has good intentions because the dopamine, the feel good drug, is raging, naturally working it's way throughout you mind. At first, you feel so good about everything and about the person you selected. However, just realize you may be fooling yourself and your partner. If you have not had many life experiences together, you cannot expect to know how you would behave in each of those situations. In terms of relationships, if you have had only one, you don't really know how different things could be. If you have had more than one, how do you feel about each? Each can teach you things about yourself, about your partner, and about your future partners. Think back about what was good and bad. Did you learn from the bad experiences? Understanding your partner in a new, deep way is the key to a better, more fruitful marriage.

One last thought: you might think the person you choose has nothing to do with financial success. Think again, my friend. Whom you choose could make all the difference. If you do choose right, you could realistically and literally become a millionaire; but if you choose wrong, you will be a pauper. Divorce can cripple people financially. Marrying the right person, with the right money values, can give you the support and encouragement you need to enable you to build a small fortune. Think about it! Be smart! Marry smart!

♀ ♂

DANA & DON

39 – Questionnaire

Deepening the Bond

The following is a series of questions to help you and your partner assess your compatibility. These are questions to help you get a discussion started in order to become more deeply aware of each other. Have fun, be honest, and enjoy getting to know your partner in a deeper and more meaningful way.

1. **CULTURE AND SPECIAL INTERESTS**
   a. Is music, art, sports, or any other interest a major part of your life?
   b. How often do you participate in any of these interests?
   c. Are you aware of any music, art, sport, or other passion that brings out emotions within you? Which ones bring pleasure, sadness, or are energizing?

2. **MONEY**
   a. Do you believe in saving money? Do you have any savings?
   b. If you get a bonus at the end of the year, what percentage goes towards debts accrued, towards retirement, or purchasing?

    d.   Do you avoid debt? Or is debt a part of life?

    e.   What is your minimum payment toward debt? Is it more than minimum?

    f.   Have you been described as frivolous, frugal, or both, depending on the situation?

    g.   Do you purchase the latest technology?

    h.   Does your partner discourage or encourage your spending?

    i.   Would you need your partner to help budget?

    j.   Is there full disclosure on spending, expenses, debt, etc. with your partner?

3. SEX

    a.   Do you have sex once a day, once a week, once a month, or only on special occasions?

    b.   Do you and your partner experiment in the bedroom, allowing each of you full sexual satisfaction?

    c.   Do you need some stimulation or emotional connection before you have sex?

    d.   Do you or your partner use sex as a weapon or leverage?

    e.   Is pornography acceptable?

4. POLITICS

    a.   What is your political affiliation?

    b.   What is the main reason for this affiliation?

    c.   How do you feel about the following:

        i.   Global warming?

        ii.   Pro-life/pro-choice issues?

        iii.   Same-sex marriage?

        iv.   Welfare and the health care system?

5. VACATIONS AND TRIPS

    a.   When planning a vacation, how do you decide

where to go? What are your preferred travel destinations?

b. How far in advance do you need to be at the airport?

c. How much time in advance do you spend planning your trip? Do you sift through websites, talk to travel agents, trying to get that perfect deal? How much time before your trip do you spend on planning?

d. Do you have every minute planned out, or do you leave it up to chance?

6. MAJOR EVENTS AND INFLUENCES

a. Have you had a defining moment in your life that shifted your outlook?

b. Has there been an influential person in your life? Who and how did they influence you?

7. COMMITMENT

a. Would you care for your partner if they became disabled or handicapped? If your partner was laid off and could only find a job far below their last salary or wage, would you be supportive?

c. If you discover infidelity in your marriage, how would you proceed?

8. LIVING DAY TO DAY

a. What is your daily routine?

b. How will your routine change over time?

c. What things will you refuse to change in the future?

d. Is there any daily routine your partner does or doesn't do that annoys you?

e. Are you a morning or a night person?

f. Do you leave clothes, food, and clutter around?

    g.   Do you leave a TV on even if no one is watching it?

9. FRIENDS

    a.   Do you feel you should go out for a girls' or guys' night out on a regular basis?

    b.   Do you feel it is OK to tell your friend(s) intimate details about your relationship with your partner?

    c.   Do you have a best friend?

    d.   Does your partner like your friends? Why or why not?

10. VALUES, CHARACTERISTICS AND PERSONALITY TRAITS

    a.   Do you believe in honesty all the time, or do you believe that a little white lie won't hurt anyone?

    b.   When is it OK not to tell the truth?

    c.   Do you do the right thing even when no one is looking?

    d.   Do you find others have to wait for you?

    e.   Do you do what you say you're going to do in a timely matter?

    f.   Are you self-disciplined?

    g.   Are you a tenacious person?

    h.   Do you often blame others or circumstances when things don't go well?

    i.   Do you welcome more responsibility or do you become easily overwhelmed?

    j.   Pick one value that you believe represents you?

    k.   What characteristics make someone heroic in your eyes?

    l.   Is your partner a pessimist, an optimist, or a realist?

    m.   Do you view your partner as a giver or a taker?

    n.   Do you find it hard to say no or set boundaries?

    o.   When you are faced with a major decision, how do

you handle it? Do you mull it over and think of every single possible alternative and every pro and con, or do you make a quick decision and hope for the best?

p. Do you enjoy reading self-help books, fiction books, non-fiction books, magazines, and newspapers, or is the only reading you do the texts on your phone?

q. Does your future include having the best house and the best car on the block?

r. What are your strengths?

s. What are your weaknesses?

t. Were you an excellent, average, or bad student? What do you think made you either excel or lose interest?

u. Do you get antsy when you are in a restaurant and are not attended to right away?

v. Have you ever had road rage? If yes, what happened?

w. Do you prefer to give your time or money to a charity?

x. Does it make you feel good doing things or buying things for your partner?

y. When someone or something bothers you, will you put up with it forever by holding it inside? Do you put up with it for a period of time and then blow up, or do you let the person know right away, even if it is a stranger in a public place?

z. Is there something, if found out about the other partner, that would cause the relationship to end for you?

aa. Do you have to have pets in your life? If yes, what kind would they be?

bb. Are you quite happy sitting with the remote on the couch, or do you have to be active every minute you are not at your job?

cc. Do you purposely seek out or avoid socializing different races ethnicities or religions outside of your own?

11. RELATIONSHIP

a. What do you think makes a relationship work?

b. How do you and your partner make up or repair the connection after an argument?

c. Do you admire and would you like to emulate a relationship between another couple you know? What is it about their relationship you like?

12. WANTS AND NEEDS

a. Can you identify the one thing in your life that you could not live without or could not live with?

b. If you were to be granted one wish, what would you wish for?

c. Pick one thing you desire most out of life?

d. Make a list of all the things that you think you could not live without.

e. Make a list of all the things you absolutely cannot have in your life.

f. Combine lists "d" and "e" and call this your NEEDS list.

g. Make a list of the things that you would like to have, but think you could live without.

h. Make a list of the things you wish were not in your life, but could live with.

i. Combine lists "g" and "h" and call this your WANTS list.

13. CAREERS/JOBS

a. Do you feel that anybody who is not working is just not looking hard enough?

b. Do you consider your work a career or a job?

c. Are you happy in your work?

d. Are you happy with the job your partner has?

e. Are you interested in what your partner does?

f. Have you ever been fired or laid off? If yes, what happened?

g. If your child was performing in a school play and your boss wanted you to put in overtime, would you stay at work or attend the play?

h. How would you feel if your partner had a more prestigious or better job than you?

i. Have you transitioned from job to job to find a career that satisfies you?

j. Have you ever been called a workaholic?

k. What would you do if you or your partner could not find work for over a year?

14. CHILDREN AND PARENTING

a. Is one of you going to stop working after the child is born?

b. If yes, how many years will they not work? Will that person ever go back to work? If one of you does not work, did you know that, by law, the other one becomes financially liable for that person in most jurisdictions, even in a divorce?

c. How do you feel about the following subjects in regards to parenting?

   i. Discipline?

   ii. Hitting? Not at all, a little slap, or a major spanking once in a while.

     iii. Yelling?

     iv. Education? Private or Public? College? Tutors?

     v. Socializing your child? What does that mean to you and your partner?

     vi. Many friends or select friends?

d. Why do you think you would be a good mother or father?

e. Do you see yourself copying things that your parents said or did?

f. Do you and your partner want to have children? If yes, how many? When do you want to start?

g. If you found out that either you or your partner could not have children, would you do anything and everything necessary to have a child or choose not to have children? If you would do anything, does that mean having a surrogate?

h. How do you feel about abortion or sterilization?

i. Will the father be in the delivery room to see the birth of the child?

j. Is having a child the single most important thing in your life?

k. Would you divorce if you could not have children together?

l. How much time will each of you take off to care for the children when they are born?

m. Do you expect your parenting style to be like that of your parents or other person?

n. Do you think you will want to be the child's friend or their parent?

o. What is your parenting style?

p. Is it important for you to give your kids the things you did not have growing up? What are those things?

q. What are the priorities in life that you want to impress upon your children?

r. Do you feel that girls and boys should be raised differently? If yes, in what way?

s. How will you show affection to your children?

t. Do you have a monetary goal to reach before having children? What is it? How long would you wait to achieve that goal?

u. Do you have an idea about the cost for formula, diapers, car seats, high chairs, cribs, strollers, and other infant-care items?

v. Do you plan on saving money for your children's financial security or educations? If not, how do you plan on paying for their education?

w. Would you go into debt to provide toys, clothing, computers, and other high-tech items?

x. How important is it for your child to wear brand-name clothing?

y. Do you plan on enrolling your child in sports training, tutoring, music lessons, or other similar things?

z. If you could live on just one person's income, which one of you would stay at home? If one of you stays home, how long would that last? Till the child begins Kindergarten? Till the child finishes high school? Or throughout the college years?

aa. Do you plan to give your child a cash inheritance?

15. THE PAST

a. Is there anything in your past that you regret?

b. If there was one thing that you could change in your past, what would that be?

c. Are there things in your past that you will not share

with your partner, or are you completely open with everything?

d. Do you think there is something your partner is hiding from their past?

e. What is the most embarrassing moment in your life? Why was it embarrassing for you?

f. Did you ever want revenge against anyone while you were growing up? If yes, why?

g. Describe a memory from your childhood that did not feel good and still bothers you.

h. Describe the types of children you grew up with. How would they describe you?

16. PARENTS AND FAMILY

a. Is there anyone in the family you do not talk to?

b. Were your parents divorced? Should they have been? If they were divorced, what do you think was the reason?

c. Do you and your partner want to treat each other the way your parents treated each other?

d. Were you raised to believe that marrying was a primary goal in life?

e. Are your parents opinionated about how you should live while married?

f. Does your partner feel you are too attached to, or too easily influenced by, your parents?

g. Generally speaking, are you more likely to take advice from your partner or your parents?

h. If you have a disagreement with your partner, would you take solace with your parents?

i. If you had a problem with your in-laws, do you believe that it is your partner's issue and it should be resolved by your partner?

   j.   Do you feel that you have to behave, dress, or talk differently around your in-laws?

   k.   Do you believe your in-laws have too much influence on your partner's thoughts and actions?

   l.   What are your childhood memories of your mom?

   m. What are your childhood memories of your dad?

   n.   Did they get along, or do you remember fights and arguments all the time?

17. PREVIOUS RELATIONSHIPS AND MARRIAGES

   a.   How do you feel about your partner having contact with their ex?

   b.   Would you be OK with some of the money you earn going towards alimony or child support of your partner's ex?

18. SPIRITUALITY, FAITH, AND RELIGION

   a.   Do you and your partner share the same faith?

   b.   Will you be an active member of your religious community?

   c.   Will you follow all the areas of your faith?

   d.   Do you believe GOD has a plan for you?

19. FINAL QUESTION – "THE BRASS RING"

   a.   Do you believe it's possible to strengthen your relationship and therefore live happily ever after?

Reviewing these questions over time can help you discover new thoughts and feelings. This exercise can be explored over and over again. In fact, reviewing them on special anniversaries could offer an opportunity to renew your love and connection.

About the Author:

Dana Greco

DANA GRECO is a licensed clinical social worker, psycho-therapist, and certified mediator. She holds a master's degree from Fordham University, a post-master's certification from the Ackerman Institute for Family and Couples, and serves as an expert forensic clinician for New York's Family and Supreme Courts. Dana has been a specialist family therapist with Memorial Sloan-Kettering in New York City, a social worker for the public school system, and has held numerous workshops for families in crisis.

In addition to her private practice, Dana has raised two daughters in Manhattan and is the author of *Please Don't Buy Me Ice Cream: a Child's Rules for Priceless Parenting*.

Dana Greco and Don Desroches are the co-founders of The Mediation and Family Counseling Group, and of Family Advocates Information and Resources **(FAIRNYS.org)** to help families in need due to family court and divorce laws in New York State. They are also the hosts of the radio show "New Beginnings," which inspired the writing and research for this book.

To learn more, go to **www.mediationandcounseling.com.**

About the Author:

Don Desroches

DON DESROCHES pulls together the material in this book from hundreds of experiences and stories while mediating divorces with partner Dana Greco, as part of his professional caseload, and from his personal experiences in marriage and relationships.

Don made the decision with Dana to write this book to try to save marriages before they got to divorce. In addition to volunteering as a coach for over 20 years, Don has volunteered his time with many different organizations to help children and families.

He has over 20 years of experience mediating and facilitating in the Financial Services industry, providing him the ability to understand the complexities of each individual's finances during mediation sessions.

Dana Greco and Don Desroches are the co-founders of The Mediation and Family Counseling Group (**www.mediationandcounseling.com**) and of Family Advocates Information and Resources (**FAIRNYS.org**) to help families in need due to family court and divorce laws in New York State. They are also the hosts of the radio show "New Beginnings," which inspired the writing and research for this book. In addition to volunteering time at FAIRNYS.org, he volunteers at other similar non-profit organizations, Fathers and Families New York, Inc., and Families Civil Liberties Union, where he serves as a family advocate.

CONSCIOUS COUPLING ™

providing:

- counseling services
- couples workshops
- retreats
- online resources
- membership practicing
  conscious coupling

www.consciouscouplingservices.com

*The authors are available
for speaking engagments.*